KU-079-816

Warwick Studies in Industrial Relations

Social Stratification and Trade Unionism

Warwick Studies in Industrial Relations

General Editors: George Bain, Hugh Clegg,
Allan Flanders

979UBE

Social Stratification and Trade Unionism

A Critique

George Sayers Bain

Deputy Director
SSRC Industrial Relations Research Unit
University of Warwick

David Coates

Lecturer in Politics
University of York

Valerie Ellis

Research Associate
Oxford Centre for Management Studies

HEINEMANN EDUCATIONAL BOOKS
LONDON

Heinemann Educational Books Ltd

LONDON   EDINBURGH   MELBOURNE   TORONTO   SINGAPORE
JOHANNESBURG   AUCKLAND   IBADAN
HONG KONG   NAIROBI   NEW DELHI
KUALA LUMPUR

ISBN 0 435 85126 8

© George Bain, David Coates, Valerie Ellis, 1973

First Published 1973

Published by
Heinemann Educational Books Ltd
48 Charles Street, London W1X 8AH

Printed in Great Britain by
Northumberland Press Limited, Gateshead

Editors' Foreword

Warwick University's first undergraduates were admitted in 1965. The teaching of industrial relations began a year later, and in 1967 a one-year graduate course leading to an M.A. in Industrial Relations was introduced. At about the same time a grant from the Clarkson Trustees allowed a beginning to be made on a research project concerned with several aspects of industrial relations in selected Coventry plants.

In 1970 the Social Science Research Council established three Research Units, one of them being the Industrial Relations Research Unit at Warwick. The Unit took over the Coventry project and developed others, including studies of union growth, union organization, occupational labour markets, coloured immigrants in industry, ideologies of 'fairness' in industrial relations and the effects of the Industrial Relations Act.

This monograph series is intended to form the main vehicle for the publication of the results of the Unit's projects, of the research carried out by staff teaching industrial relations in the University, and, where it merits publication, of the work of graduate students. Some of these results will, of course, be published as articles, and some in the end may constitute full-scale volumes. But the monograph is the most apt form for much of our work. Industrial relations research is concerned with assembling and analysing evidence much of which cannot be succinctly summarized in tables and graphs, so that an adequate presentation of findings can easily take too much space for an article. On the other hand, even with a major project which will in the end lead to one or more books, there is often an advantage in publishing interim results as monographs. This is particularly true where the project deals, as do several of the industrial relations studies at Warwick, with problems of current interest for which employers, trade unionists and governments are anxiously seeking solutions.

The first four titles in the series were based on case studies, although each of them used the cases to develop theory. This study of social stratification and trade unionism, written by the Deputy Director of the Unit and two outside colleagues, is an essay in industrial relations theory based on a critical review of the pertinent literature. It examines the presuppositions about the relationship between class and trade union membership which have shaped a number of studies of trade unions and trade unionists, and which underlie many current notions about the nature and behaviour of trade unions. By revealing the inadequacies of many of these presuppositions, it hopes to clear the way for more fruitful studies in the areas of union growth and behaviour, areas in which the Unit has research projects under way.

George Bain
Hugh Clegg
Allan Flanders

Contents

Contents

Preface

There is now a considerable body of literature in which patterns of union growth and character are explained primarily by reference to various aspects of the system of social stratification. Indeed, such writings have come to exert a major influence on academic and popular thinking about trade unionism. But after undertaking separate pieces of research into various aspects of unionism, especially among white-collar workers, we have come to feel that this literature is less than adequate in several respects. This study is the result of our joint effort to make clear our feelings of unease.

Although we draw upon our own research findings, our major purpose here is not to report on them in any detail. This has been done elsewhere (*8; 36; 63*).* In our view, the time has come to take stock of our existing knowledge, to assess it, and to try and suggest new lines of development. Consequently, this study is primarily a survey of the existing literature on the link between social stratification and trade unionism, and it is at times highly critical of the existing material in the field. Indeed, paradoxically, most of the criticism is directed towards that part of the literature which is undoubtedly

---

* The numbers within the brackets refer to the sources which are listed at the end of this study. Where there are several consecutive references to the same source, the source number in the bibliography is given with the first reference, and only the page numbers are given with the suceeding references.

the most sophisticated. For it is precisely the apparent plausibility of this literature which necessitates a serious consideration of its validity.

Just because this is a survey of the literature, we have attempted as far as possible to quote directly from the relevant texts in order that the reader can interpret for himself the arguments which are being assessed. Moreover, since the literature which is surveyed is international in nature, an attempt has been made to include examples from a wide range of Western countries. But since we are more knowledgeable about Britain than about other countries, and since a good deal of the most significant writing on social stratification and trade unionism is British, developments in this country tend to be emphasized.

There were several drafts of the manuscript, and this necessitated a great deal of typing. We are very grateful to Muriel Stanley, Hélène St Martin, and Hilary Williams for doing it so efficiently and patiently.

Our greatest debt is to our academic colleagues who gave us the benefit of their comments and criticism. They include Eric Batstone, Peter Bowen, Hugh Clegg, Joe England, Allan Flanders, Alan Fox, Bob Fryer, Richard Hyman, Bob Price, and Monica Shaw. In expressing our gratitude to them, we stress that they do not necessarily share any of the opinions we express. For these and any shortcomings which may remain in spite of their efforts, we alone are responsible.

George Bain
David Coates
Valerie Ellis

I

Introduction

White-collar unionism, the main focus of this study, has only recently received any detailed attention from social scientists. But it is by no means a new phenomenon. In such countries as Australia, Britain, France, Norway, Sweden, and the United States, white-collar workers began to form and to join unions during the last half of the nineteenth century, and by the beginning of the twentieth century these unions were generally established on a fairly stable basis.* Trade unionism has continued to expand among these workers, and today there is a considerable degree of white-collar unionism in most Western countries. But regardless of the extent of unionism among white-collar workers, it is generally not as great as that among manual workers. Only 13 per cent of white-collar workers are unionised as compared to 56 per cent of manual workers in the United States, 24 per cent as compared to 42 per cent in Germany, 30 per cent as compared to 81 per cent in Australia, 38 per cent as compared to 53 per cent in Britain, 58 per cent as compared to 65 per cent in Norway, and 70 per cent as compared to over 80 per cent in Sweden.†

* See Martin (*161*, pp. 1–11) for Australia, Routh (*195*, pp. 173–84) and Pickard (*180*) for Britain, Crozier (*43*, pp. 100–112) for France, Fivelsdal (*64*, pp. 82–3) for Norway, Nilstein (*173*, pp. 268–73) for Sweden, and Kassalow (*127*, pp. 317–30) for the United States.

† For the United States see Solomon and Burns (*214*, p. 148) and Kassalow (*127*, p. 338). For Germany see Hartfiel (*102*, p. 158, table 4). For Britain see Bain and Price (*9*, p. 378, table 11). For Australia the figures have been calculated from data given by Martin (*159*, p.

This difference in the degree of white-collar and manual unionism has encouraged speculation about the determinants of the growth and character of unionism among white-collar workers, and has led many theorists to concentrate on factors which are believed to distinguish these workers from manual workers. There is no shortage of explanations. Almost every conceivable determinant has been listed, and often without any indication of its relative importance.* The most common and persistent school of thought, however, holds that the key determinant is the different positions of white-collar and manual workers within the social stratification system. The purpose of this study is to examine this school of thought. The specific focus of the study is white-collar unionism because it is in this context that the link between stratification and unionization has been most frequently and most clearly made

I. THE CONCEPTS

The discussion of the relationship between stratification and unionization will be facilitated if the meanings of the various concepts used in this study are first made clear. There are several such concepts: white-collar and professional employees, union growth, union character, and social stratification.

White-Collar and Professional Employees

'White-collar employees' have been defined in terms of their method of payment, their place of work, the nature

95). The white-collar figure for Norway is from Fivelsdal (*64*, p. 83), while the manual figure is from the Personal Correspondence of the Authors, letter from Egil Fivelsdal 21 April 1972. For Sweden see Nilstein (*173*, p. 261). These figures should be used cautiously in making comparisons between countries because the definitions, the quality of the data, and the years for which they were collected vary from one country to another.

*For a critical discussion of some of these determinants, see Bain (*8*).

of their work, and the type of dress they wear to work.*
Similarly, the usual approach to defining a 'professional'
is to assemble a 'constellation of characteristics' which in
one way or another seem to suggest a 'profession'.† The
characteristics most commonly assembled include
specialized knowledge and skills acquired by formal
training, control of the work performed, altruistic service in the interests of society, and honourable and
ethical action in performing the work.

The main problem with the 'constellation of characteristics' approach to definition is that different people
choose and emphasize different characteristics with the
result that the list of occupations offered as 'white-collar'
or 'professional' varies from one writer to another. In
order to encompass the variety of definitions offered, the
terms 'white-collar' and 'professional' are generally used
in this study in their widest possible sense. Where a particular theory depends upon a specific definition, however, then it is used in examining the validity of that
theory.

Union Growth

Union growth is a quantitative concept: it is something
which can be measured. There are primarily two ways
in which this can be done: in terms either of *actual*
union membership or of the *density* of union membership. The density of union membership is given by the
following formula:

---

* See Bain and Price (*10*) for a review of the major theories which
have been advanced in an attempt to evolve a logical and consistent
definition of a 'white-collar employee'.

† See Cogan (*37*) and Habenstein (*96*) for a review of some of the
ways in which 'professional' has been defined. Hughes (*115*) has argued
that the significant question to ask about occupations is not whether
they are professions, but to what degree they exhibit the characteristics
of professionalization. This has led scholars such as Hickson and
Thomas (*104*) to try and develop scales of professionalization.

$$\frac{\text{Actual Union Membership}}{\text{Potential Union Membership}} \times 100$$

This study, like most others, uses this latter basis for the measurement of union growth. By using the density of union membership rather than actual union membership, one of the most obvious causes of union growth, changes in potential union membership, can be controlled for in the subsequent inquiry into the relationship between union growth and social stratification. The density of union membership has also been referred to as the percentage organized, real membership, the degree of unionization, and the completeness of organization, and these terms are used interchangeably throughout this study.

Union Character

Many writers have mentioned but few have developed what Blackburn has called the 'much neglected but essential concept' of union character (*15*, p. 7). Robert Hoxie has written of 'union viewpoint and action' and of the 'general functional and structural character' of unionism (*112*, pp. 52, 55). Routh has referred, without elaboration, to the 'quality' of union activity (*195*, p. 202), Crozier to its 'character' (*43*, p. 90), and Kassalow to its 'form' (*127*, p. 363). C. Wright Mills has alluded to the 'shape and policy', the 'political character', and the 'mentality and direction' of white-collar unionism (*170*, pp. 316, 314), and Martin to its 'changing character' (*161*, p. 18). And Richard Lester has interchangeably used 'essence', 'essential features', 'character', and 'objectives and operations' to analyse unions as they 'mature' (*142*, pp. 12, 19, 21, 129).

Fewer writers have attempted to isolate the elements of character in order to give a rigorous and explicit definition of the concept. The 'essential features' of union 'character' for Lester, though never explicitly given, appear to be union government, the quality of leadership, and the degree of militancy (pp. 22–3). For Rawson they seem to be affiliations to the wider labour movement, industrial militancy, and political activity (*187*, p. 196). For Lipset they are 'ideology, class solidarity, tactics, organizational structure, and patterns of leadership behaviour' (*148*, p. 77). Shostak refers to the 'character' or 'personality' of a labour organization as 'the core of attitudes members and leaders assume toward the principal union problems and the rationale they offer for these attitudes' (*208*, pp. 128, 8). Fughrig, in defining a 'quasi-union', isolates the key characteristics of a trade union to be 'legal prerogatives, organizational discipline, equalitarian sentiment, and faith in the moral justification for strikes' (*70*, p. 127).

The most rigorous definitions of union character have been given by Lockwood and Blackburn. Lockwood argues that the character of a white-collar union can be traced with respect to such general questions of policy as

> whether it is to be registered as a trade union, whether it is to be associated with the wider trade union movement made up preponderantly of manual workers, whether it is to be affiliated for political action with a party, whether it will seek parliamentary support and if so in what form, and whether, finally, it will resort in the last instance to strike action in the defence of its members' interests (*150*, p. 155).

For Blackburn the main features of a union's character are 'externally, its policy (including objects), practices, associations, and the public image it has created; and internally, its organisation and structure', and he suggests similar indices to Lockwood's for measuring union character (*15*, p. 18).

Many of these definitions of union character as well as the general question of what comprises an adequate definition of union character will be considered in greater detail later in the study. But it should already be clear that there is no general agreement as to the exact meaning of the concept. Hence it will be used here in two different ways. First, each statement on union character will be tested in the light of the particular definition adopted in that statement. Second, the more general arguments about the uniqueness of the character of white-collar unions and professional associations will be considered against two major dimensions of character: organizational goals and patterns of organizational behaviour.

Social Stratification

There is no consensus on the nature and determinants of social stratification. On the contrary, the character of social stratification is a major issue of debate in modern social science. The literature is characterized by competing definitions of such key categories as 'class' and 'status' and by considerable terminological and conceptual confusions.* To adequately chart a course through this debate is far beyond the limited purpose of this study and would involve detailed consideration of material and events far removed from trade unionism. But it is both possible and necessary to make a number of points about the nature of social stratification.

There is widespread agreement that social stratification involves

> the division of a population into strata ... between [which] there are relationships ... of inferiority and superiority ... Stratification is in fact a means of regulating access to what the economist calls 'scarce goods', by which he means not just material objects of consumption ... but 'psychic' and 'immaterial' satisfactions, such as

* A perusal of any of the basic texts on the subject will confirm this statement. See, for example, Gordon (*90*), Barber (*12*), and Owen (*178*).

the distribution and receipt of prestige, as well as the distribution and receipt of material objects (*251*, pp. 283–4).

It is also worth stressing Runciman's point that

we are indeed dealing with stratification and not merely with differentiation; or in other words, the metaphor of high and low must be appropriate. This question too has sometimes led to confusion. But it should be self-evident that when speaking of either wealth, prestige or power we are speaking of something which by definition admits of the notion of ranking. Of course, there are other human attributes which admit of ranking, such as physical height, but from a sociological standpoint, these are individual, not institutional, differentiations. What needs to be clear at the outset is both that economic class, status and power admit of ranking and that these rankings, however they are measured or described, are institutionalised or, in Rousseau's distinction, 'conventional' as opposed to 'natural' (*197*, p. 106).

The literature on social stratification has been characterized by the use of categories initially generated by either Marx or Weber. When discussing the relationship between class consciousness and trade unionism, the literature considered in this study has confronted what is one of the central problems of Marxist analysis. In doing so, however, it has not operated within a Marxist analytical framework, but has adopted either implicitly or explicitly the Weberian categories of 'class' and 'status'. Weber defines 'class' to refer to any group of people who have the same

typical chance of a supply of goods, external living conditions, and personal life experiences, in so far as this chance is determined by the amount and kind of power, or lack of such, to dispose of goods or skills for the sake of income in a given economic order (*72*, p. 181).

And it is generally taken to cover such basically economic aspects of stratification as size and source of income, degree of job security, and opportunities for upward occupational mobility. Status is concerned with a person's position in the hierarchy of prestige in the society at large, with what Weber calls the 'social estimation of honor' (p. 187). It is based on such social factors as consumption patterns and resulting life styles, family background, education, and occupation. Because this study attempts, at least in the first instance, to assess each theory within its own terms of reference, it too makes use of the distinction between class and status.

Finally, it is necessary to distinguish between stratification variables and associated variables. 'By *associated* variables', to quote Gordon,

> we mean behavioral categories which are not, in themselves, hierarchical but which are produced by the operation of stratification variables, and which in turn contribute to the dynamics of stratification (*90*, pp. 239–40).

For example, voting Conservative, reading *The Times*, and purchasing clothes at Harrods may be associated with superior positions, but these behaviour patterns are not themselves hierarchical by nature. Neither is trade unionism. To what extent it is an associated variable is what this study is attempting to find out.

II. THE BASIC MODEL

The theorists who have linked social stratification and trade unionism differ considerably in the complexity of their arguments. Some have simply correlated union growth and character with one or more of such dimensions of position in the stratification system as income, job security, education, social origins, occupational prestige, and self-placement. In doing so, they have not attempted to explain why such a relationship exists. They seem to have assumed that the causal mechanism of the relationship is so self-evident that it need not be spelt out.

But other theorists have been more explicit. They have claimed that the workers' position in the social stratification system generates a certain picture or image of industry and the wider society which shapes their attitudes to trade unionism. In effect, they have postulated the existence of an intervening variable—social imagery—which links the independent variable—social position—with the dependent variables—union growth and union character.

Figure I gives a schematic description of the basic

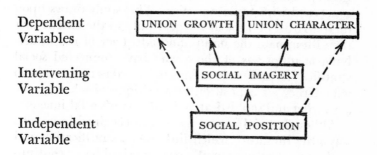

Dependent Variables

Intervening Variable

Independent Variable

UNION GROWTH UNION CHARACTER

SOCIAL IMAGERY

SOCIAL POSITION

FIGURE I

The Relationship between Trade Unionism and Social Stratification

model offered, either implicitly or explicitly, by those writers who have linked trade unionism and social stratification. This description constitutes the general form of the argument normally advanced, and no one person can be said to offer it in its entirety. Rather, as will become clear as the study progresses, writers generally stress only certain of the relationships it subsumes. But when taken as a whole, the body of literature on trade unionism and social stratification operates within the framework of the relationships laid down in this model. The broken lines represent the direct links made between social position and unionization by some writers;

the solid lines represent the more sophisticated version in which the intervening variable—social imagery—is made explicit.

III. SOCIAL IMAGERY

Types of Social Imagery

Because so few students of trade unionism and social stratification have explicitly considered the intervening variable of social imagery, it is necessary to refer to the writings of sociologists who were not themselves directly concerned with trade unionism. This study draws upon their writings on social imagery only to the extent that they illuminate the nature and adequacy of the under- lying assumptions of those who have connected social stratification and trade unionism. It makes no attempt to offer either an exposition or a critique of what is now a growing and sophisticated discussion of social imagery.

Although social images have been classified in various ways, the literature which links social stratification and trade unionism is generally characterized by its continu- ing reliance on a simple polarity of the kind first estab- lished in the pioneering studies of Popitz in Germany (*183*), Willener in Switzerland (*246*), and Bott in Eng- land (*19*). These demonstrate, according to Goldthorpe and Lockwood, that

> One 'polar' type of image is that of society as being sharply divided into two contending sections, or classes, differen- tiated primarily in terms of the possession or non-posses- sion of power (the 'dichotomous' or 'power' model). Contrasting with this is an image of society as comprising an extended hierarchy of relatively 'open' strata differen- tiated primarily in terms of prestige (the 'hierarchical' or 'prestige' model) (*84*, p. 146).

In their own work, Goldthorpe and Lockwood have characterized the 'prestige' model as 'radical individual- ism' and the 'power' model as a 'solidaristic collectivism'.

In addition to having different means for achieving goals, these two orientations differ in the type of goals to be achieved. The latter takes solidarity and collectivism as terminal goals possessing intrinsic value, while the former prefers the goals of individualism and success (pp. 153–4).*

Runciman has expressed essentially the same view although he labels the two orientations 'egoism' and 'fraternalism'. The egoist seeks his career advancement through individual effort rather than by making 'common cause with others like him'. A hypothetical example is a junior business executive balked of promotion who is continuously and resentfully aware of the senior directors of his firm. He

> compares his position with theirs, he aspires to become one of them, and he sees this prospect as a perfectly feasible one in terms of his expectations or demands. He has no feeling that the social categories either of junior executives or of businessmen in general are lower in rewards, or esteem, or influence than they should be, nor does he feel himself a member of any other group which is ill-treated by his society as a whole. But he feels intensely deprived relative to the position of other people whom he regards as deserving no greater recognition that himself. He is, therefore, relatively deprived only in terms of his personal situation; there may be others in the same situation with whom he shares some kind of fellow-feeling, but his achievement of what would assuage his feeling of relative deprivation is in no way bound up with theirs (*196*, p. 32).

The fraternalist, on the other hand, can best be illustrated by a factory worker who feels that he is grossly underpaid.

---

*It is necessary to stress that Goldthorpe and Lockwood, unlike the other writers discussed here, do not operate with such a simple polarity of social imagery. They recognize the existence of several social images (*152*).

He is conscious, and even militantly conscious, of belonging to the working class. He has no ambition to rise above his fellows. But he feels that he and all those like him are insufficiently rewarded both in money and status by the society to whose welfare they are contributing by their work. He feels relatively deprived as one of a class whose members all share the same conditions of life and employment (p. 32).

Prandy has also isolated two images of the social structure—a 'status ideology' and a 'class ideology'. Those who possess a 'status ideology' see society as

a set of superior and inferior grades in which every member accepts the validity of the status criteria, and thus his own place within the hierarchy. Status stratification is essentially harmonious, in the sense that it arises out of an acceptance of the authority structure. Individuals can compete with one another to raise their own status, but the validity of the criteria by which status is measured, the bases of legitimation, is not questioned (*184*, p. 37).

Those who possess a 'class ideology', on the other hand, see society as being stratified according to the possession or non-possession of power; they reject the claims of those with power and believe that this power must be challenged (p. 174).

The images of society described by the above writers obviously contain a number of similar elements, and these are summarized in Table I. Those who adopt the image of society variously referred to as the prestige model, the hierarchical model, radical individualism, egoism, and a status ideology see the social structure as being completely open, with a hierarchy of strata which can be scaled on the basis of individual merit and effort. Those who fail to reach the 'top' do so because of personal inadequacies rather than through any structural limitations to mobility inherent in the social system. In consequence, those holding such a social image tend to be concerned with both the level and the stability of their position in the status hierarchy. Those who possess the social image variously referred to as the power model, the dichotomous model, solidaristic collectivism, fraternalism, and a class ideology see the relations between clearly defined social classes in terms of conflicts of power and interest, and see 'social mobility' in terms of the collective advancement of one class at the expense of another. In short, the major distinction between these social images is that between two basic dichotomies: harmony versus conflict and individualism versus collectivism.

The Link Between Social Imagery and Social Position

Several of the theorists who have isolated these two basic images of society have argued that the one tends to be held by white-collar workers while the other is generally held by manual workers. Popitz, Willener, and Bott found, to quote Goldthorpe's and Lockwood's summary of their work, that

> The 'power' model is that most frequently approximated in the images of working class persons—that is, wage-earning, manual workers. The 'prestige model' on the other hand, is that most frequently approximated in the images of middle class persons—that is, salaried or independent non-manual workers (*84*, p. 146).

Similarly, Runciman has argued that

> one of the strongest arguments for drawing the principal line between manual and non-manual workers is the well-attested difference in the traditional values and ethos of the two strata—a difference which at once derives from and helps to preserve the other differences of which I have been speaking.
>
> This difference can be put in one way by saying that working-class norms are 'collectivist' and middle-class norms 'individualist'; this is one reason why the relative deprivations felt by working-class people are more likely to

TABLE I
Social Imagery

ELEMENTS OF SOCIAL IMAGERY	TYPES OF SOCIAL IMAGERY	
	Prestige Model Hierarchical Model Radical Individualism Egoism Status Ideology	Power Model Dichotomous Model Solidaristic Collectivism Fraternalism Class Ideology
1. Mode of Stratification	Hierarchy of social categories placed in order according to various consensual criteria of prestige. *(HARMONY)*	Two interacting social classes with differential power. *(CONFLICT)*
2. Relationship Between Categories Or Classes	Harmony between social groups with consensus over existing distribution of power, facilities, and rewards. *(HARMONY)*	Conflict between classes with rejection of existing distribution of power, facilities, and rewards. *(CONFLICT)*
3. Mode of Ascent Through the Social Hierarchy	Individual ascent according to individual merit. *(INDIVIDUALISM)*	Collective ascent by means of collective action. *(COLLECTIVISM)*
4. Relationship Between Ends and Means	Individual goals and individual means seen as intrinsically valuable. *(INDIVIDUALISM)*	Collective ends and collective action seen as intrinsically valuable. *(COLLECTIVISM)*

be what I have called 'fraternalistic' and those felt by middle-class people 'egoistic' (*196*, p. 50).

Prandy does not define precisely where the boundary lies between those holding a status ideology and those holding a class ideology. He begins by arguing that white-collar employees, unlike manual workers,

> do not 'believe in' class, certainly not in any way which involves class conflict....
> Class theories of stratification cannot deal adequately with these middle-class groups, for the concern of such people is with status, a quite different form of stratification (*184*, p. 35).

But he later formulates his argument in a more general way by pointing out that these ideologies are ideal types which form the poles of a continuum of images. He thinks it probable that those higher in the stratification system, such as professionals, possess a status ideology; that those lower in the social hierarchy, such as manual workers, possess a class ideology; and that those in the middle of the hierarchy, such as lower-level white-collar workers, possess a mixture of ideologies. But 'in any particular situation', he expects 'there to be a tendency for an individual's views to be either predominantly of a class or a status type' (pp. 38, 174).

To summarize, there is a measure of agreement amongst certain theorists concerned with the link between social stratification and trade unionism. Most writers have simply operated with the dichotomy of 'class' and 'status' images. But a few have argued that these two basic social images are ideal types which form the poles of a continuum of images, and the extent to which either of these dominates the workers' outlook will depend upon their position in the social stratification system. Whether the imagery is seen as a discrete or a continuous variable, however, all agree in associating the 'status' pole with white-collar workers and the 'class' pole with manual workers.

Implications Of Social Imagery For Trade Unionism

The various types of social imagery are claimed to have different consequences for union growth. A class ideology* is seen as being consistent with unionism in that it stresses collective means to collective goals and conflicts of interest between powerful employers and weak employees. In Sykes' view,

> Trade unionism is based upon unity and collective action. Trade union members must surrender their rights of individual action and competition in the cause of unity. As a result the industrial worker has become accustomed to regard anything which causes individual competition and disunity as bad. He does not seek the advancement of the individual as such but the advancement of the group of industrial workers of which he is part. Any preferment or promotion for the individual tends to create disunity, hence men are taught not to compete but to co-operate. In consequence the good trade unionist supports his trade union right or wrong, and whether the case at issue affects himself as an individual adversely or not. He knows that if he acted on his interests as an individual each time his union would be powerless (222, p. 177).

A status ideology, on the other hand, is believed to be inimical to unionism. Those who possess such an ideology are assumed to see themselves as individuals capable of progressing through society unaided and without protection. They regard trade unions as an intrusion into a highly personal employment relationship, as being necessary only for those who do not have sufficient determination and merit to succeed on their own.

---

* Since Prandy has most explicitly related social imagery to trade unionism, his terminology—class and status ideologies—is henceforth used to refer to the two basic social images.

The low degree of unionism among white-collar workers, for example, has generally been attributed to the fact that most of them are believed to possess a status ideology. Strauss notes that for white-collar workers to join a union

> means abandoning hope; it means showing hostility to the boss (whom they may dream of as a close associate and personal friend); it also means throwing away all opportunity to forge ahead on merit (*217*, pp. 74–5).

Sykes argues that clerks

> want to 'get on' as individuals; they want promotion. They act individually and set the highest value on individuality; they think it right and proper to do what benefits them personally, not what benefits clerks as a whole. Thus their interests lie in raising their own status as individuals, not working through a trade union to raise the status of all clerks. The way in which they do this is by competing for promotion in the office, and by improving their individual status through securing educational or professional qualifications at night school or by private study. This entails dealing directly with the employer and striking individual bargains with him on pay and conditions (*222*, p. 177).

Similarly, Burns feels that white-collar workers are 'suspicious' of unions because they 'focus attention on the welfare of the group and tend to forget the individual in the group' (*28*, p. 71).

But white-collar and other workers who are believed to possess a status ideology nevertheless join unions. In doing so, however, it is generally argued that they do not adopt a class ideology. White-collar workers join unions, in Strauss's view,

> not because they reject their middle-class aspirations, but because they see unionism as a *better way* of obtaining them. In other words, they look on the union as a means of obtaining dignity, prestige, and control over environ-

ment, things which are denied them by the increasingly bureaucratic organization of the modern office (*217*, p. 81).

Similarly, Mills argues that unions are usually accepted by white-collar workers

> as something to be used, rather than as something in which to believe. They are understood as having to do strictly with the job and are valued for their help on the job.... Acceptance of them does not seem to lead to new identifications in other areas of living.
>
> .   .   .
>
> In the union or out of it, for it, against it, or on the fence, the white-collar employee usually remains psychologically the little individual scrambling to get to the top, instead of a dependent employee experiencing unions and accepting union affiliation as collective means of collective ascent. This lack of effect of unions is of course linked with the reasons white-collar people join them: to most members, the union is an impersonal economic instrument rather than a springboard to new personal, social, or political ways of life.
> ... Unions, 'instrumentally' accepted, are alternatives to the traditional individualistic means of obtaining the traditional goals of success. They are collective instruments for pursuing individual goals; belonging to them does not modify the goals, although it may make the member feel more urgently about these goals (*170*, pp. 308–9).

These writers would seem to assume, at least implicitly, that by joining a union the white-collar workers' position in the social stratification system may be pulled simultaneously in opposite directions. More specifically, they assume that white-collar workers may find themselves being pushed upwards on the economic dimension of stratification but being pulled downwards on the status dimension. To quote Mills once again:

> If the unions raise the level and security of the em-

ployees' income, at the same time they may lower the level and security of prestige. For in so far as white-collar claims for prestige rest upon differences between themselves and wage-workers, and in so far as the organizations they join are publicly associated with worker organizations, one of the bases of white-collar prestige is done away with (pp. 311–12).

In other words, trade unions are sometimes assumed to present white-collar workers with a 'trade-off' problem: they have to calculate what income and other economic benefits are worth in terms of prestige. Or, to put it another way, they have to calculate the optimum combination of these two 'social goods' which will maximize their position in the social stratification system.

Indeed, the instrumental reasons for joining are assumed to have to be very strong before white-collar workers overcome their principled objections to unionism. That is, white-collar workers are assumed to accept unions only as a last resort, when all other options for improving their situation are closed. This is taken to be in direct contrast to many manual workers who are assumed to possess a class ideology, and, in Burns' words,

> look upon unions as having ideological value. They tend to accept unionism on the basis of principle and in terms of the positive values of group interest, group action and group identification (29, p. 35).

In fact, some writers assume that all manual workers view unionism in this way, and there is a general tendency in the literature on the subject to contrast the instrumental view of unions held by white-collar workers with the principled commitment to unionism of manual workers.

The different social images which manual and white-collar unionists are assumed to hold are claimed to result in the latter being less active and involved in union affairs, and in the character of manual unionism being significantly different from that of white-collar union-ism. Rawson claims that manual unions differ from white-collar unions* primarily because the members of the former

> approximate to a single social class, in this case the working-class.... [They] not only have common economic interests but occupy a particular place in the community and share common values and aspirations (*187*, p. 200).

White-collar unionists, on the other hand, are assumed to form an amorphous and heterogeneous category, com-prising various sectional interests. This diversity of interests is reflected in the development of narrowly-based unions which are concerned only with the sectional interests of their own members. Rawson recog-nizes that his argument may be oversimplified, but maintains that manual 'unions differ from other interest groups because, and to the extent that, it approaches the truth' (p. 200).

Similarly, for Allen, the methods of white-collar unions are distinct because their members cannot readily dispense with the 'middle class values' which 'have led them in the past to denigrate crude industrial action' (*4*, pp. 172–73). And in attempting to explain why white-collar unions are different, Strauss claims that

> the one important special characteristic of these unions is the middle-class background and orientation of their members. This fact is fundamental to an understanding of why white-collar workers unionize, to the success of organ-ization drives, to high participation in union activities,

---

* Rawson insists that the groupings he isolates are those unions whose members identify with the working class and those unions whose members identify with the middle class, and that this distinc-tion is 'similar, but not identical' to the manual/white-collar dis-tinction (p. 198, n. 7). But, as Martin points out, 'the groupings he apparently thought he ended up with do not differ greatly from those obtained by using the manual/non-manual distinction, and in the course of his article he slid now and again towards a statement of the distinction in those terms' (*160*, p. 131).

to satisfactory negotiations and relations between office and shop unions (*217*, p. 73).

He goes on to point out that many white-collar workers 'are possessed by the Horatio Alger dream of working up from office boy to president', and, if this dream is not realized to some extent, then they may turn to unions. But 'because these middle-class dreams are not completely dissipated, white-collar unions have a character of their own' (p. 74).

Professional employees are often assumed to stand close to the top of the social hierarchy, and hence they are believed to hold particularly tenaciously to the status ideology. In Prandy's view,

> The ideology of these groups is on the whole favourable to management, and even where they have accepted the instrumental value of a union it is usually only with reluctance. Some see unionism as undesirable but inevitable, others as only necessary because management has forced it upon them by its 'aberrations'. They feel that they are not treated as they deserve and that this is undesirable for the whole of society as well as for themselves. They see, or rationalize, their own interests as the interests of all, and their attitude towards collective bargaining is essentially one of helping management to see reason— to preserve it from its own follies. There is thus a great emphasis on co-operation, which finds its expression in the official objects of the associations as well as in the attitudes of the members (*184*, pp. 142–3).

Moreover, this status ideology is claimed to be reinforced among professionals by a 'professional ethic'. This ethic is propagated by many professional bodies, and it emphasizes the unity of interest and harmony of purpose between professionals—whether employees, self-employed, or employers—which derives from their being members of a common professional group. Indik and Goldstein claim, for example, that 'over and above the attitudes common to these categories, an additional barrier to acceptance of unions has operated among engineers—the proposition that collective action is incompatible with their professional status' (*119*, p. 211).

This is assumed to result in professional unions and associations differing significantly not only from manual unions but also from white-collar unions. Goldstein argues that professional workers are members of the middle class, and hence

> Their definition of various aspects of trade unionism, and the role of unions in general is based on the perspective gained in responding to the expectations of the middle class members with whom they work and among whom they live. It might be expected, therefore, that professionals would have a different orientation towards important elements of the trade union process than industrial workers, springing from important differences in their socio-economic and ecological locations (*79*, p. 324).

Indeed, after analysing several examples of professional unionism, he concludes that 'salaried professionals, because of their educational background, their occupational culture, and their position within the firm, have produced a form of trade unionism that differs significantly from traditional trade unionism' (77, p. 200).

The argument is given a somewhat different formulation by Prandy. He claims that the class and status ideologies 'do not just exist in individuals' but are 'institutionalized into two different types of organization—professional associations and trade unions' (*184*, p. 31). 'Trade unions are class bodies—they bargain with employers; professional associations are status bodies—they bestow a qualification and seek to maintain or enhance its prestige' (p. 44). This difference in orientation underlying the two types of organization is held to explain differences in their behaviour. Trade unions recognize a conflict of interest with employers and engage in collective bargaining and militant action; professional associations do not.

Thus for Prandy

> A trade union is unlike any other occupational association in that its function is to bargain with employers on behalf of employees. In thus giving expression to a conflict of interest it is a class association, and by joining it its members have to some extent given up a large part of their status ideology in favour of a class ideology.

.   .   .

> The existence of a trade union, therefore, is taken as an indication of class attitudes (pp. 42–3).

The notion that trade unionism is a reflection of class consciousness has been further developed by other writers. Lockwood claims that the 'class-conscious feeling of the blackcoated worker is reflected in the degree to which his union identifies itself with the Labour Movement' (*150*, p. 197). And Blackburn argues that 'it is an important feature of unionisation that it may be taken as an index of class consciousness' (*15*, p. 9).

IV. CONCLUSION

Although the arguments which this study is setting out to evaluate are complex, they can nevertheless be briefly summarized. The workers' position in the social stratification system is assumed to produce a certain picture or image of industry and the wider society. The various images which different social positions are thought to generate are classified into two basic types—a class ideology and a status ideology. The class ideology which most manual workers are believed to possess is favourable to unionism; indeed, unionization is claimed by some to be an indication of class consciousness. The status ideology which most white-collar workers are believed to possess is unfavourable to unionism. These different social images are held to explain why manual workers are generally more highly unionized than white-collar workers. They are also claimed to result in the character of white-collar unionism differing significantly from that of manual unionism. For when white-collar workers do unionize, they are believed to carry with them certain elements of the status ideology which affect the behaviour of their unions. Professionals are believed to hold particularly tenaciously to the status ideology with the result that their associations and unions are significantly different not only from manual unions but also from white-collar unions.

This body of argument is analysed in two stages. Chapters 2 and 3 consider the relationship between the independent variable, social position, and the two dependent variables, union growth and union character. Chapter 4 then considers the validity of the premise upon which these relationships are based, namely the association between social position and the intervening variable, social imagery. The final chapter tries to draw the various parts of the analysis together and suggest ways in which future research in this area might fruitfully develop.

2

Social Stratification
and Union Growth

The previous chapter has described how certain writers
have attributed to white-collar workers a particular
social imagery which has negative implications for trade
unionism. The extent to which this social imagery
dominates the outlook of various white-collar groups is
claimed to depend upon their position in the social
stratification system. The exact nature of the relationship between social position and trade unionism has not
always been made clear. But with respect to union
growth, there are basically two hypotheses, each of which
has a static and a dynamic version.

I. THE HYPOTHESES

Hypothesis A

The first hypothesis states that the lower the workers'
position in the social stratification system or the further
it falls the more likely they are to unionize; conversely,
the higher the workers' position or the further it rises
the less likely they are to unionize. This argument will
be referred to as Hypothesis A.

Although the static version of this hypothesis probably
dominates popular thinking about union growth, Lipset
is one of the few academic writers who has explicitly advanced it in the literature on the subject. In his view,

the most important correlation between support of the
left or of trade unionism and any other variable is posi-

tion in the stratification structure. That is, the more privileged a group is in terms of income or status, the more likely it is to be conservative in its politics. The same pattern would appear to hold up for the appeal of trade unions as well (*147*, p. 3).

The dynamic version of Hypothesis A is much more widely supported by academic writers. Shlakman has argued that it was the depression of the 1930s which confronted the American white-collar worker

> inescapably with the contradiction between the realities of his existence and his folklore.... The white collar class was made up of wage-earners, though they liked to call themselves salaried employees. They were dependent on an employer for their livelihood. They were more and more being employed in groups that were growing in size. While they felt themselves to be of the middle class and tried to behave accordingly, it was becoming much harder to maintain the conventional differentials between their standards of living and those of production workers. Hence tangible evidence of superior social status was less than satisfactory. The frontal assault on living standards during the long depression finally set the stage for the rise of white collar unionism.
>
> .   .   .
>
> The resistance to organization, based on myth and illusion, slowly began to yield to the influence of technology and economic reality (*207*, pp. 16, 26).

A virtually identical analysis to Shlakman's has been provided for Great Britain by Klingender (*134*) and Allen (*3*). To quote Allen, white-collar workers are 'members of a permanent employed class in exactly the same way as manual workers', but as a result of their social aspirations they 'became involved in a great social pretence' and 'formed an image of themselves which bore little resemblance to economic realities'. But they 'are increasingly practising trade-unionism because they know they are losing their status and recognize that the causes are institutional ones'.

Many writers would reject the notion advanced by Shlakman and Allen that the status preoccupations of white-collar workers are 'unreal', 'illusory', or 'false', and that at least by implication their reluctance to unionize is 'irrational'. But they would nevertheless agree that the 'status proletarianisation' of white-collar workers causes them to unionize. For example, Strauss has argued that

> in recent years white-collar work has become increasingly routine, opportunities for promotion have declined, and in many cases wages have dropped below the factory level. White-collar workers—particularly those with long service —often feel that their legitimate expectations have been disappointed. Then they turn to unions (*217*, p. 74).

Similarly, Sturmthal has suggested that

> unionism may be an instrument by which discrepancies between traditional status and that based upon present function are maintained for as long as possible. Thus white-collar groups whose status is primarily based upon tradition and whose position in the plant (and consequently in society) is declining are more susceptible to unionism than groups whose status is confirmed or enhanced by the new technology and labor market balance. White-collar unions then are regarded by the first group as defensive organizations to maintain the threatened status quo. In particular, they may be used to resist the 'proletarianization' of white-collar workers or their inclusion in a blue-collar bargaining unit (*221*, p. 389).

Hypothesis B

The second hypothesis is the obverse of the first: the lower the workers' position in the social stratification system or the further it falls the less likely they are to unionize; conversely, the higher the workers' position

or the further it rises the more likely they are to unionize. This argument will be referred to as Hypothesis B.

No explicit statement of the static version of Hypothesis B appears to exist in the literature on union
growth. But some remarks of C. Wright Mills give at
least tacit support to the dynamic version of this theory.
He has argued that as white-collar workers are increasingly proletarianized, there may be a 'status panic'—
a frantic drive to protect the remaining bases for separate consideration. The white-collar worker may 'seize
upon minute distinctions as bases for status' and this
may 'operate against any status solidarity among the
mass of employees, ... lead to status estrangement from
work associates, and to increased status competition'
(*170*, p. 254). Where this occurs, white-collar workers
will presumably be hostile to unions 'for in so far as
white-collar claims for prestige rest upon differences between themselves and wage-workers, and in so far as the
organizations they join are publicly associated with
worker organizations, one of the bases of white-collar
prestige is done away with' (p. 312).

Sturmthal has advanced the converse of the dynamic
version of Hypothesis B. The above statement by him
suggested that workers are more likely to unionize if
their social position is declining. But he has also argued
that

> The opposite situation—functionally rising status con-
> trasting with low status tradition—may also lead to
> unionization. For such groups unionization serves pri-
> marily as a device to resolve the conflict between tradition
> and the present. Organizations then may be quite short-
> lived. They fulfill their mission to adjust status, wages,
> and working conditions to the new situation and then
> disappear (*221*, pp. 389–90).

This argument has also been advanced by Kassalow (*126*,
pp. 42–3; *127*, pp. 354–5) to explain the unionization of
certain professional groups such as teachers, airlines

pilots, and journalists in the United States, and by Reynaud (*189*, pp. 151–7) to account for the unionization of certain technical and managerial grades in France.

II. TESTING THE HYPOTHESES

A very general evaluation of the two hypotheses can easily be given. Clearly, both cannot be universally valid since the one is the obverse of the other. Conceivably, both might be valid in specific instances; each might explain the behaviour of different groups of workers. But this possibility raises the awkward problem of explaining why two groups which share the same position in the stratification system should behave differently with respect to union membership. Those such as Sturmthal who have simultaneously advanced both theories have not provided such an explanation which, in any case, would need by its very nature to rely upon a factor other than the groups' position in the stratification system.

To provide a more detailed evaluation of the two theories is more difficult. For there is no generally agreed measure or indicator of position in the social stratification system. There are broadly three ways in which a group may be assigned a position in the stratification system: by referring to some 'objective' characteristic such as its income, by gauging the amount of prestige accorded to it by others, and by asking the group to place itself. Objective, accorded, and subjective measures may produce different results. To overcome this difficulty, all three types of measures will be employed in testing the two hypotheses.

Objective Measures

Many characteristics of a group may be used as an objective measure of its position in the stratification system. The full range of possibilities cannot be investigated here. There is room to examine only those objective measures which have most frequently been related to the propensity to unionize. These include social origins, education, security of employment, income, and authority.*

Social origins. 'The social status of an occupation depends in part', as Lockwood has observed, 'on the social origins of the individuals who enter it'. An occupation which recruits its members from higher social strata of the population tends to have a higher status than those which recruit from lower social strata. The social origins of an occupation's members is 'at once an index and a cause of its social standing' (*150*, p. 106).

Several social scientists have examined the relationship between social origins and union membership. Lipset and Gordon analysed the data from a 1949 sample of manual workers in the San Francisco Bay area and found that the downwardly mobile—that is, manual workers with non-manual fathers—were less likely to be union members than the non-mobile. But they then examined the backgrounds of the downwardly mobile males in greater detail and found that the greater the degree of downward mobility the more likely they were to be union members although the number of cases and the differences among the various groups were too small to be statistically significant (*149*, pp. 492–3). Curtis replicated the Lipset-Gordon study among a sample of manual workers in Detroit and obtained similar results

---

* Several studies have also found a relationship between the propensity of workers to join unions and the extent to which they work in close proximity to unionized workers or have trade unionists among their friends and relatives. Such patterns of association are sometimes taken as an indication of position in the social stratification system, but this cannot be done within the context of this discussion. For to take union membership as being related to, or an index of, position in the stratification system is to assume the very point which is being tested. In any case, as Bain has argued (*8*, pp. 43–6, 84–6) there are good reasons for believing that the correlations which some researchers have established between these patterns of association and union membership are spurious.

although they were not statistically significant at the 5 per cent level (*45*).

Curtis also examined the relationship between social origins and union membership among a sample of male non-manual workers in Detroit and found that the upwardly mobile were more likely to be union members than the non-mobile and that the greater the degree of upward mobility the more likely this was to be the case (p. 70). Lipset analysed the data generated by a survey of labour mobility in six major American cities in 1951 and found that both male and female clerical workers and sales personnel who came from manual homes were much more likely to be union members than those who did not (*147*, pp. 21–2). In Britain, Phillipson found that draughtsmen who had manual fathers were more likely to be union members than those who did not (*179*, pp. 279–80). Blackburn found that there was a tendency among male bank clerks for those from higher-status homes to be in the staff associations or nothing, while the lower the status of their background the more likely they were to be in the National Union of Bank Employees (*15*, p. 198).

The findings of these studies are so varied and permit so many interpretations that they could obviously be used to support either of the above diametrically opposed theories. But it would be unwise to use them in this way for their very diversity makes them unconvincing. Moreover, some of these same studies, as well as others, have failed to establish a relationship between union membership and social origins. Kornhauser analysed the data generated by an American national public opinion survey in 1952 and found no relationship between the social origins of manual workers and union membership. She also analysed the data provided by the survey of labour mobility in six major American cities in 1951. Although Lipset found a relationship in this sample between social origins and union membership for clerks and sales personnel, Kornhauser could not find a similar relationship for manual workers (*135*, p. 43). Goldstein and Indik found no significant correlation between social origins and union membership among the American professional engineers they surveyed (*80*, pp. 366–7). The relationship between union membership and social origins which Blackburn found among his sample of British male bank clerks did not exist among his sample of female bank clerks. Nor did it hold for either males or females among his second sample of bank clerks (*15*, p. 198). Similarly, the relationship between union membership and social origins which Phillipson found for draughtsmen did not exist for the clerical and administrative workers in his sample (*179*, pp. 279–80).

In addition to their contradictory findings, these studies suffer from methodological shortcomings. Many of the samples are small and something less than random.* More serious, none of the studies controlled for all the other factors which might influence workers to join unions. For example, none controlled for size of firm or for the way in which the firm was administered, and none but Blackburn's even controlled for industry.† It may be, as Lipset and Gordon have frankly admitted (*149*, p. 499, n. 14), that many of the non-unionists were working in small paternalistically-administered firms in which they had close interpersonal relations with their employers, and that this rather than their social origins explains their reluctance to join trade unions.

Even if these studies were unanimous in their findings and free of methodological shortcomings, they would still be very difficult to interpret. For example, several of the studies found that upwardly mobile white-collar

* The researchers themselves admit this. See Phillipson (*179*, pp. 164–70); Blackburn (*15*, pp. 64–5); and Lipset and Gordon (*149*, p. 499, n. 14).

† The importance of such variables for unionization has been pointed out by Lockwood (*150*, pp. 138–50) and Bain (*8*, pp. 72–81).

workers were more likely to be union members than the non-mobile. Do the upwardly mobile unionize as the dynamic version of Hypothesis B suggests because their status is rising, or do they unionize as the static version of Hypothesis A suggests because their status, as measured by their social origins, is lower than that of the non-mobile? It is difficult to answer these and other questions 'without', in the words of Lipset and Gordon, 'considerably more data on the subjective correlates of these background variations' (p. 493).

Clearly, those who have argued that union membership and social origins are related have not proved their claim. This failure on their part does not in itself permit the opposite conclusion that such a relationship does not exist. Such a conclusion, however, is supported by the very nature of the union membership patterns in various countries. To take a few random examples, the density of white-collar unionism is 13 per cent in the United States, 38 per cent in Britain, and 70 per cent in Sweden (*supra*, p. 1). Within the United States it is 82 per cent in the post office, 58 per cent in transportation, and 2 per cent in finance and insurance (*214*), while within Britain it is over 80 per cent in national and local government, 23 per cent in paper, printing, and publishing, and less than 4 per cent in chemicals (*8*, pp. 21–39). Even within the same occupational group there is considerable variation from one industry to another; in Britain draughtsmen are 80 per cent unionized in vehicles, 50 per cent in engineering, and less than 6 per cent in chemicals (p. 35). It is extremely doubtful if the social origins of white-collar workers vary sufficiently or systematically enough to account for more than an insignificant amount of this variation in union density.

Education. Many people would agree with Mills that education is 'the white-collar employee's "capital", the major basis of his prestige' (*170*, p. 269). Thus if the above hypotheses were valid, it would not be unreasonable to expect a relationship between education and union membership. Unfortunately, the relationship between these two variables cannot be adequately tested because of a lack of data. But, as with social origins, it is most improbable that education varies sufficiently or systematically enough to account for more than an insignificant amount of the variation in union membership patterns. Moreover, the amount and type of education received by occupational groups is correlated very highly with their social origins (*150*, pp. 119–20; *68*). Hence the influence of education upon the propensity to unionize is probably much the same as the influence of social origins, namely—little, if any. Similarly, the amount of education required to pursue an occupation is highly correlated with its prestige (*211*). But, as is demonstrated later (*infra*, pp. 44–53), occupational prestige is not very closely related to unionization, and hence unionization is unlikely to be closely related to education.

What empirical research there is tends to support this conclusion. Kornhauser analysed the data provided by an American national public opinion survey in 1954 and found no systematic relationship between education and union membership among male manual workers (*135*, p. 41). Seidman and Cain, unlike Kornhauser, controlled for occupation and studied unionism among professional engineers and chemists employed by an oil refinery in the American Midwest; they found that there was a slight positive association between level of qualification and union membership (*202*, p. 244). But Goldstein and Indik could not find a significant relationship between education and union membership among a much larger sample of American professional engineers (*80*, p. 366).

Employment security. Security of employment is also an important indicator of position in the stratification system. Employment security was perhaps the most significant difference between manual and non-manual work, as Lockwood has pointed out, 'for, although it fell short of the full independence which comes with property, job-security did constitute a partial alternative to ownership, conferring on the clerk a relative immunity from those hazards of the labour market which were the lot of the working classes' (*150*, p. 204). The depression demonstrated that white-collar employees are not immune to unemployment. But there has been so little unemployment in the majority of Western countries over most of the period since the Second World War, especially among white-collar employees, that it is unlikely to account for at least post-war patterns of union growth.

Empirical research tends to support this conclusion. Ashenfelter and Pencavel found that union membership in the United States between 1900 and 1960 was responsive only to fairly large changes in unemployment; the effect of small changes was almost negligible (7, p. 444). In Britain, Hines found that between 1893 and 1961 aggregate unemployment and union membership were significantly correlated only in the sub-period 1893–1912 (*107*, p. 234), and he could find no consistent or convincing relationship between these two variables at industry level between 1948 and 1962 (*108*, pp. 70–4).

Income. An important determinant of the life chances of most individuals and hence of their position in the stratification system is the size of their incomes. Thus if the above hypotheses were valid, income and union membership should be quite closely related. Many people have claimed that they are. But very few of them have bothered to offer any evidence in support of their claim. Those who have examined the available evidence have found that it lends little support to either of the above hypotheses.

In analysing the data generated by the 1952 American national public opinion survey, Kornhauser found that male manual workers with higher incomes were more likely to be union members than those with lower incomes. But she did not feel that these findings provided her with a basis for arriving at 'a definitive conclusion concerning the independent effect of income on union membership'. For it was not possible to control adequately for the effects of other variables which might have affected the relationship. Moreover, income 'may be viewed as a potential consequence as well as a potential determinant of union membership'. Thus even if income and union membership were related, 'it would still be necessary to ascertain whether income differences result from or cause variations in membership rates, an issue that cannot be settled with the data at hand' (*135*, pp. 41–2).

Lockwood found in his study of clerical workers that

> There is little demonstrable connection between unionization and 'economic' position in the narrow sense of level of income, and degree of job-security. Those clerks with the least income and security of tenure are not those with the greatest degree of organization. On the contrary, it is among the more highly paid and secure clerical population that the degree of unionization is highest (*150*, p. 150).

His findings tend to contradict Hypothesis A, although they might be thought to lend some support to Hypothesis B. But this is doubtful. For as Lockwood himself has demonstrated, differences in the degree to which various clerical groups have unionized is to be explained not by differences in their incomes but primarily by differences in their work situations (pp. 138–49). Thus this relationship between unionization and income would seem to be a product of chance factors, or conceivably, the higher incomes might result from the higher degrees of unionization rather than vice versa. But this is a possibility which Lockwood did not examine.

Bain analysed the relationship between the earnings of

white-collar workers and the extent to which they were unionized in British manufacturing industries (*8*, pp. 51–63). He could find no relationship between the absolute earnings levels of white-collar workers and the degree to which they were unionized. This finding tends to contradict the static version of both the above hypotheses. Nor could he find any significant relationship between the degree to which white-collar workers in manufacturing industries had unionized and the extent to which the differential between their earnings and either those of manufacturing manual workers or those of white-collar workers as a whole had been narrowed. These findings tend to contradict the dynamic version of both the above hypotheses.

Authority. Relation to the exercise of authority is among the more fundamental aspects of position in the stratification system. Hence it is not surprising that proponents of the above hypotheses have tried to link this variable to unionization. For example, Prandy has argued that joining a union is more likely for those who do not share, or expect to share later through promotion, in the exercise of authority as part of management, and even more likely for those whose employment situation emphasizes their subordinate position. 'The important factors here are not merely market situation—low income and lack of opportunity, but also work situation —such things as strict supervision, lesser personal control over work, organization in large, impersonal work groups, and so forth' (*184*, pp. 169–70, 174–5).

The evidence which Prandy offers in support of his thesis is unconvincing. He found among the members of the Institution of Metallurgists that those doing technical work were more likely than those doing administrative work to want the Institution to 'do more' to improve the status and salaries of metallurgists (p. 100). Similarly, he interviewed members of the Engineers' Guild in the Merseyside area and found that while those doing administrative work were two-to-one against the Guild engaging in collective bargaining, those doing technical work were equally divided (pp. 120–1). Both these pieces of evidence assume that those engaged in technical work are more likely than those engaged in administrative work 'to be cut off from authority and to feel themselves cut off' (p. 95). But it is not clear exactly how 'technical' and 'administrative' are defined, and relatively little *a priori* reasoning and no empirical evidence are offered to substantiate the assumption that those doing the former type of work are more likely than those doing the latter to be in subordinate positions. Even granted this assumption, the relationships portrayed by these two pieces of evidence are not based, at least in the case of the Engineers' Guild, upon very large or representative samples, and, by Prandy's own admission, are not very marked or significant (pp. 100, 120–1).

Prandy also analysed the recruitment patterns and work experience of qualified scientists and engineers in the North-West Region of the Association of Scientific Workers between 1955 and 1960. He found that there were many more recruits from electrical engineering than from chemicals, and concluded that this is accounted for by differences in the type of work performed by the two groups. In his words,

Although the great majority from both were employed in technical work, that is, they were not part of management, in electrical engineering many more were in work which would emphasize the fact. Their jobs were often close to those of actual production, such as testing, drawing up specifications, designing, or even production itself. This type of work is likely to involve organization in larger work groups, lesser control over the job, more supervision, and more routinization—in all, those conditions which will emphasize their subordinate positions (pp. 183–4).

He claimed that 'this situation is fairly common in the

electrical engineering industry, especially on the elec-
tronics side', and that it accounted for the degree of
unionism among scientists and engineers being generally
higher in this industry (2.5 per cent) than in chemicals
(1.0 per cent) (pp. 151–2).

This piece of evidence is particularly weak. The fact
that there are more recruits from electrical engineering
than from chemicals may be explained by the industrial
distribution of employment; perhaps electrical engineering employs more scientists and engineers in the North-
West than does chemicals. Prandy claimed that 'if anything, one would expect to find more members from the
chemical industry in this area' (p. 151). But he offered
no evidence to support this claim which, in any case, it
would be difficult to do since there are no published
data on the geographical distribution of the scientific
and technical labour force. Similarly, he did not give
the source of his data which show that the degree of
unionism among scientists and engineers is generally
higher in electrical engineering than in chemicals, and
a survey carried out in 1964 suggests that the reverse is
true.*

Even granted that the differential in membership density is as Prandy claimed, his explanation of it is unconvincing. An analysis of the employment of a small
number of recruits in the North-West is an unrepresentative basis upon which to make generalizations regarding the nature of work in various industries. Even
granted that these generalizations might be true, Prandy
was unable to offer any independent evidence which
proved that the nature of work determines unionization.
In an attempt to do so, he interviewed members from
five Merseyside branches of the Association of Scientific

---

* Bain (*8*, p. 35) found that for Great Britain as a whole the degree
of unionization among scientists and technologists in 1964 was 12.5
per cent in chemicals as compared to 3.9 per cent for engineering and
electrical goods.

Workers. Although he found that the majority of them were engaged in technical work, that is they were not managers, he admitted that

> Unfortunately, the limited situation being considered here does not produce sufficient evidence to support the hypothesis that those nearest to production are the ones most likely to unionize. Branch B does provide some, since 7 of its 9 members are engaged either in production or in process control, and it is the most successfully organized. In Branch A, the largest, however, most of the qualified members are doing research and development (p. 158).*

It is also worth remembering in this connection that it has not been the least-skilled manual workers who have been most ready to join trade unions, but those possessing the most skill and personal control over work. Similarly, it has not been those white-collar workers such as clerks and office-machine operators who have the most routine and monotonous work who are the most highly unionized in Britain and several other countries, but those such as draughtsmen and journalists who have the more creative and interesting work.

Even granted that those engaged on work closely related to production tend to unionize, it does not necessarily follow that this is because their subordination is

---

* Prandy argues that:

This should not be taken as contrary evidence. In the first place, it probably means that this particular company uses qualified men much less in direct production work. Secondly, in this field it is not always easy to draw a line between development and design work, and the conditions under which the former is carried out differ greatly from those of the research ideal.

But he does not offer any evidence from this particular company to justify these statements. Even granted that these findings should not be taken as contrary evidence, they can hardly be taken as evidence supporting his thesis that those engineers and scientists engaged on work closely associated to production are more likely to unionize than those who are not. And he offers no other independent evidence on this point.

emphasized by the characteristics which Prandy saw as associated with this type of work. For example, he found that several employees he interviewed joined the Association of Scientific Workers because their firm had been taken over by a larger company and they feared redundancies might ensue. He went on to conclude that:

> Their reasons for joining are very much as one would expect. That is, in terms of the hypothesis put forward, their employment experience has made them aware of their divorce from management (p. 161).

Has it really done this, or has it simply made them insecure? Prandy was clearly reading a lot into the responses when he claimed that because people who are insecure, dissatisfied with their incomes, or frustrated with the routine nature of their jobs join a union, they do so because these factors have made them aware of their subordinate positions. Moreover, characteristics such as insecurity are not the monopoly of those in subordinate jobs closely associated with production. In the example Prandy cited, it was those in research and development who felt most insecure and joined the union and not those technical personnel on the production side. In fact, it is the continued employment of superordinates no less than that of subordinates which is commonly jeopardized by a takeover.

The evidence which Prandy offers clearly lends little support to his thesis. But other researchers have found evidence which might be taken as supporting his contention that joining a union is more likely for those who do not expect to share in the exercise of authority through promotion to management positions. C. Wright Mills claimed to have found 'a close association between the feelings that one *cannot* get ahead, regardless of the reason, and a pro-union attitude' among a group of white-collar workers in the United States (*170*, p. 307).

British researchers have pointed out that teaching and the civil service have been characterized by 'a policy of recruitment from outside at two or more levels, with little or no opportunity for those recruited at low level to surmount the internal barriers blocking their promotion'. They claimed that as a result:

> 'Elementary' school teachers, and civil servants without a university training who entered the clerical or executive classes, have had such poor chances of upward job and social mobility that their efforts to improve their lot have inevitably taken the form of creating powerful interest groups restricted to those whose promotion was virtually barred in this way. As the lower salariat often attracted socially aspiring individuals for whom the blockage of their upward mobility was especially frustrating, they often became the leading spirits in the formation and running of such organizations (*129*, p. 322).

Sykes found that almost all of the male clerks in the sales office of a Scottish steel company wanted promotion and felt they had a reasonable chance of obtaining it, but only a few approved of trade unionism for clerks. Later, most of these clerks joined a trade union. Sykes then interviewed them again and found that as a result of the company introducing a management trainee scheme many of the clerks no longer felt that promotion to management level was a real possibility. He suggested that the changed attitude of these clerks towards their promotion prospects explained their changed attitude towards trade unionism (*223*, pp. 307–10).

These studies are too limited in scope to allow any firm conclusions to be drawn regarding the effect of restricted promotion opportunities on union growth. At least they do not support Sykes's claim that 'there is evidence for an association between opportunities for promotion and trade unionism among clerical workers generally' (pp. 308–9). Nor can it necessarily be assumed that workers with poor promotion prospects unionize because they are denied the opportunity to participate in the exercise of authority. An equally plausible interpretation is that they unionize because they are denied the opportunity to 'get ahead', 'to improve their lot', to obtain better jobs in the sense of higher salaries and more favourable working conditions.

Even granted that the blockage of promotion opportunities is favourable to unionization because it emphasizes subordination, it is obviously not a necessary condition. Promotion channels were relatively open in British banking, but a considerable degree of unionization was nevertheless possible (*150*, pp. 149–50). Similarly, British draughtsmen have long been a highly unionized occupational group, yet their promotion prospects have been quite good and highly valued.*

Even those who successfully obtain positions of authority are not thereby necessarily prevented from unionizing. Employees in the public sector of Britain and many other countries are unionized regardless of their position in the authority structure. For example, the 'administrative class' of the British civil service enjoys a very authoritative position but is nevertheless very highly unionized. Many European countries also have a high degree of unionization among foremen and supervisors in the private sector of the economy. Indeed in France, these unions are often better organized and more militant than many manual unions, and one union, the General Confederation of Supervisory Employees (Confederation Generale des Cadres), includes in its ranks some management personnel in virtually the highest executive levels (*125*, p. 770). And Soffer has shown that managerial and supervisory workers founded many of the craft unions in the United States, were among the

---

* A survey of 941 draughtsmen in 1960 showed that 'prospects of advancement' was the third most frequent advantage of the occupation (with 350 mentions), compared with 188 giving 'poor chances of promotion' as a disadvantage. See Routh (*194*, p. 9).

unions' most highly organized groups, and exerted very strong, if not dominant, influence in shaping the structure and policies of these unions (*213*).

Accorded Measures

Evidence on the objective dimensions of social stratification is somewhat scrappy and often inadequate. But what evidence there is does not lend much support to either of the above hypotheses. At least it is difficult to demonstrate that there is a convincing correlation between the degree to which workers are unionized and their position in the stratification system as measured by social origins, education, employment security, income, or authority. But the above hypotheses may still be valid. For these objective factors may not be as good a measure of a group's position in the stratification system as the amount of status or prestige accorded to it by others.

Common-sense classifications of prestige. In order to see what relationship, if any, exists between the social status or prestige accorded to an occupation and the degree to which it is unionized, Kornhauser (*135*, p. 34) analysed the data provided by a survey of labour mobility in six American cities in 1951 and by two American national public opinion surveys in 1952 and 1954. There are slight differences among the occupational classification schemes used in these surveys, but the following scheme is typical:

All nonfarm occupations
All nonmanual
Professional, semiprofessional
Proprietors, managers, officials
Clerical, sales
All manual
Skilled
Operatives

    Service workers
    Labourers*

Such a scheme is generally referred to as a 'common-sense' classification of prestige because it is based on the commonsense judgement of the constructor that the various occupational categories selected are correlated with socio-economic status, prestige, and skill.

Kornhauser found that the degree of unionization among male manual workers in both the 1951 and 1954 samples was approximately the same for skilled, semi-skilled, and unskilled workers, but much less for service workers. 'These results', says Kornhauser,

> call into question a common belief that unionization is highest among skilled workers; they also fail to support the contrary belief that the lowest ranking occupations should be easiest to organize. Given the relatively high unionization of male manual workers, differences in skill, income, and status within the manual division do not appear to be significant influences on membership rates [density]. Moreover, the single exception (service workers) to the general rule that intra-manual occupational differences are not associated with differential rates of union membership also indicates that the *rank* of a manual occupation is not currently its most significant characteristic with respect to union membership. The low membership rates of service workers probably cannot be related to occupational characteristics that lie along the skill-income-prestige (i.e., rank) dimension, for occupation groups that are higher as well as those that are lower in rank are both more highly organized than service workers. The deviant position of service workers is in all likelihood associated with the peculiar working conditions characteristic of service occupations (*135*, p. 35).

Among non-manual workers, on the other hand, Korn-

* All farm occupations have been omitted from the classification. The classification schemes in all three surveys would seem to be based on that devised by Alba M. Edwards (*60*) in the 1930s for use in the United States Census of Population.

hauser found that male clerical and sales workers, in her opinion, the 'lowest-ranking nonmanual occupational group', always had a higher degree of union membership than higher ranking groups such as professionals and proprietors, managers, and officials. 'It thus appears', says Kornhauser, 'that within the nonmanual category occupations low in income, skill, and status are more accessible to organization than are the higher ranks' (p. 36).

But, as she herself admits, this conclusion must be qualified in certain respects. To begin with, membership differences among the various non-manual occupations are much less marked for women than for men. In the 1952 sample, for example, female clerical and sales workers are barely more unionized than female professionals. In addition, male professionals are more highly unionized in the 1952 sample than male proprietors, managers, and officials, although the former are viewed by Kornhauser as having a higher social rank than the latter. Similarly, in the 1951 sample where the sales and clerical workers are separated, male sales workers are less than half as well organized as male clerical workers although the former are viewed by Kornhauser as having a higher social rank than the latter.

Another important limitation of Kornhauser's study is the impossibility of controlling for other factors which might affect union membership. In her own words,

the nonmanual occupations that are more highly unionized differ from the poorly organized occupations in other important respects besides rank. For the nonmanual occupations that are low in all the criteria of rank (education, income, prestige) are also characterized by certain working conditions that favor unionization. For example, as compared to higher level nonmanual workers, clerical workers are more likely to be engaged in easily standardized tasks, to be massed together in large numbers, and to be located in industries containing high proportions of manual workers among whom strong unions have already become established. This raises the question of whether the observed differences in membership rates should be attributed to one or the other or to both dimensions of these occupations. In all probability it is both the low rank and the distinctive working conditions of the lower nonmanual jobs that help explain their higher rates of unionization (pp. 36–7).

Even this qualified conclusion would seem to over-emphasize the impact of prestige upon unionization given the somewhat inconsistent relationship which Kornhauser found between these two factors.

The most serious weakness of Kornhauser's analysis is the 'commonsense' classification of occupational prestige which she employs. Although such schemes 'may have substantial value as a *functional* classification', as Gordon has pointed out, their 'use as either a *social status* or an *economic* index is subject to severe limitations' (*90*, pp. 226–7). Firstly, no convincing empirical evidence is presented to support the assumption that all non-manual workers possess a higher social status than all manual workers. Secondly, the ranking of the various occupational groups within the manual and non-manual categories is arbitrary and theoretically difficult to justify. Thirdly, the assumptions that each classification contains occupations of equal social status and that there is no overlapping among the categories are patently untenable. In short, to quote Gordon once again, 'all the "common-sense" classifications suffer from the rather crucial limitation that their correspondence to an economic or social hierarchy is largely assumed rather than empirically demonstrated' (p. 227).

Empirical prestige ratings. Because of the severe limitations of 'commonsense' classifications, some sociologists have attempted to establish the prestige of occupations empirically. Using somewhat varying lists and numbers of occupations, they have asked various groups to evaluate the relative ranking of these occupations.

Although these empirical prestige ratings provide a better measure of social position than 'commonsense' classifications, they nevertheless have their limitations. The raters are not always a representative sample, but are often the most available persons such as colleagues of the researcher, students, and school children. And although there is a wide measure of agreement both within and across various societies, different groups rate some occupations differently (*90*, pp. 229; 252). The occupational titles used in these studies such as 'lawyer' and 'doctor' are more specific than those used in 'commonsense' classifications, but they are still excessively broad and cover people with widely varying social positions. The newer and more esoteric occupations are wholly unfamiliar to many people in a modern industrial society, and they cannot evaluate them. Hence only the more familiar occupations tend to get included in these studies with the result that less than all the occupations are covered. Even if the familiarity problem did not exist, the use of a comprehensive and more specific list of occupations would tend to be prohibited by the very large amounts of time, money, and personnel required to evaluate such a list. Finally, even the best of these empirical rating procedures do not yield a true ordinal scale of occupational prestige in terms of say the Guttman scaling technique.* Hence in Gordon's view,

> users of occupational scales for heuristic stratification of populations for the purpose of correlating with behavior variables must be prepared to accept relatively low consistency on some items in order to have an instrument

---

* This is a statistical device for testing whether a list of items such as occupations are rated consistently in relation to each other by the different individuals in the sample. That is, it determines whether a scale is really a scale in which a certain occupation ranked, say, in number 10 position is always ranked higher than all the occupations numbered higher than 10 and always ranked lower than those numbered lower than 10. See (*93*).

that is usable at all; such an instrument may still, of course, have considerable operational value (*90*, p. 230).

But despite these deficiencies, empirical prestige ratings are among the best available indicators of accorded position in the stratification system. And if the theories outlined at the beginning of this chapter are valid, it is perhaps not unreasonable to expect some relationship between the prestige rating of an occupation and the degree to which it is unionized.

To see if this is, in fact, the case in the United States, the well-known and much respected North-Hatt N.O.R.C. scale is employed here. It is the best American scale not only because the raters were a national cross-section of the American population and ranked a relatively comprehensive list of occupations (ninety), but also because it was originally constructed in 1947 and updated in 1963.* Unfortunately, the lack of detailed and reliable union membership figures classified on an occupational basis reduces the utility of the scale for the present study. Nevertheless, there is sufficient information available to allow a few conclusions to be drawn.

Indik and Goldstein use some of the data provided by the North-Hatt study to demonstrate that the lower the social standing of an occupation the higher its degree of unionization (*119*, p. 211). But they do this in a somewhat unconvincing manner. For they have chosen only those occupational groups which support their thesis. It is true that many occupations with relatively low prestige such as coal miner (50),† dock-worker (50), truck driver (59), and plumber (65) are very highly union-

---

* The results of the 1947 survey are reported in (*175*), and those of the 1963 survey are given in (*111*).

† The figure in brackets after each occupation is its prestige score on the N.O.R.C. scale. The higher an occupation's score the higher its prestige. The scores cited are those for 1963. But the 1947 scores are very similar, and, if used here, would not necessitate any substantial change in the argument.

ized,* while many occupations with relatively high prestige such as psychologist (87), biologist (85), accountant for a large business (81), and author of novels (78) are very poorly unionized. But the reverse is equally true: occupations with relatively low prestige such as shoe shiner (34), sharecropper (42), restaurant waiter (49), filling station attendant (51), and clerk in a store (56) are very poorly unionized, while occupations with relatively high prestige such as airline pilot (86) and musician in a symphony orchestra (78) are very highly unionized. And if certain professional associations are considered to be trade unions, as the following chapter argues they should inasmuch as they have similar functions to unions, then occupations such as physician (93), lawyer (89), and dentist (88) can also be added to this list.

To look at it another way, many occupations with common prestige scores have widely different degrees of union membership. For example, an airline pilot and a civil engineer have identical prestige scores (86), as do a musician in a symphony orchestra and an author of novels (78), a railroad conductor and a travelling salesman for a wholesale concern (66), a streetcar motorman and a clerk in a store (56), and a lumberjack and a restaurant cook (55). Similarly, skilled manual workers as a group have the same prestige score as clerical and sales workers as a group.† Yet in every case the first-mentioned occupation in each pair is much more highly unionized than the second.

These findings suggest that there is no close and sys-

* Claims regarding union membership are based in a general way upon Solomon and Burns (*214*) and upon Troy (*232*). But for many of these occupational groups, detailed and reliable union membership figures simply do not exist. Nevertheless, there is fairly general agreement as to what are the poorly organized and well organized occupations, and there are probably few people who would quarrel with the statements made here regarding relative degrees of unionization.

† The scores are taken from the 1947 study and are 68.0 compared with 68.2.

tematic relationship between occupational prestige and unionization, and thus they tend to contradict the static versions of both the above theories. The dynamic versions of both theories are challenged by the work of Hodge and his colleagues (*111*, p. 329). In 1963 they replicated the North-Hatt N.O.R.C. study of 1947 and where possible the 1963 data were compared to earlier occupational prestige studies going back to 1925. They found that there had been no substantial change in occupational prestige in the United States between 1925 and 1963. Yet there were considerable changes in both white-collar and manual union membership patterns during this period (*232*). Obviously, there can be little connection between changes in occupational prestige and changes in union membership.

The data problem for Britain is the reverse of that for the United States. There is a considerable amount of information on union membership among various occupational groups, but data on occupational prestige is not as reliable as that for the United States. The major study of occupational prestige in Britain (*97*) did not use a representative sample of raters, had a relatively short list of occupations (thirty), and was carried out in 1949 and has not been updated. Nevertheless, it is sufficiently adequate to allow some conclusions to be drawn.

In general, the relationship between occupational prestige and unionization is the same in Britain as in the United States. Occupations with relatively low prestige such as road sweeper (28.9),* dock labourer (27.0), and coal miner (23.2) are very highly unionized,† while many occupations with relatively high prestige such as company director (1.6), business manager (6.0), and works manager (6.4) are very poorly unionized. But once

---

* In the British study, the higher an occupation's score the lower its prestige.

† Claims regarding union membership in Britain are generally based on Bain (*8*) and Hindell (*106*).

again the reverse is equally true: occupations with relatively low prestige such as barman (26.4) and shop assistant (20.2) are very poorly unionized, while occupations with relatively high prestige such as medical officer (1.3), executive grade civil servant (6.0), and school teacher (10.8), are very highly unionized. In Britain, as in the United States, occupations with similar prestige have widely different degrees of union membership. An executive grade civil servant and a business manager have a similar prestige rating (6.0), as do a bricklayer and a shop assistant (20.2), and a railway porter and an agricultural labourer (25.3 compared with 25.5). But in every case the first-mentioned occupation in each pair is much more highly unionized than the second.

Even more doubt is cast upon the prestige-unionization hypothesis by a more detailed examination of the British union membership pattern. For example, how does prestige account for intra-occupational differences in union membership? There are, of course, intra-occupational differences in prestige (*12*, p. 109). But do they vary in such a way as to account for the degree of unionization among draughtsmen being 80 per cent in vehicles but less than 6 per cent in chemicals, that among clerks over 20 per cent in metal manufacture but only about 3 per cent in textiles, or that among virtually all occupations being much higher in the public than in the private sector? This has certainly not been demonstrated to be so, and, to say the least, it seems highly improbable. Similarly, how does prestige account for temporal variations in union membership? Considerable powers of imagination are required to see how it can explain why the degree of unionization was over 45 per cent in 1920 but only 30 per cent in 1925, or why it was less than 23 per cent in 1933 but over 45 per cent in 1948 (*9*, p. 376). And finally, how does prestige account for the very large differences in union membership patterns between countries, especially when research has demonstrated that there is a marked degree of agreement concerning the relative prestige positions given to the same occupations in various countries (*110*).

Subjective Measures

There is obviously no clear-cut connection between the amount of prestige accorded an occupational group and the extent to which it is unionized. But perhaps the position in the stratification system which is accorded to people by others is not as important a determinant of how they act as the position which people assign to themselves. A great many interview studies have tried to ascertain people's perceptions of the stratification system at the societal level by asking them to name the class to which they think they belong.* Similarly, some studies have tried to find out people's perceptions of the stratification system at the industrial level by asking them whether they identify more with management or with workers. But very few of these studies have tried to link these class identifications or self-placements with trade union membership.

In fact, there would appear to be only three such studies. Kornhauser analysed the data generated by an American national public opinion survey in 1952, and found that among male manual workers there were 'virtually no differences between union members and nonmembers in the proportions identifying with the working or middle class, or in the proportions believing that the American economic system provides the opportunity for

---

* These studies have found that there is no strong correlation between the white-collar/manual dichotomy and the self-placement by respondents into either the working or middle classes. On the contrary, Kahn, Butler, and Stokes (*123*, p. 128) found that 68 per cent of lower non-manual workers placed themselves in the working class; this figure is roughly similar to that found by Hamilton (*100*, p. 193) for the United States, and to that found by Buchanan and Cantril (*26*, Appendix D) for a number of countries.

success to anyone who works hard (*135*, p. 45). But Lipset also analysed the data provided by the same survey and found that among male white-collar workers union members were much more likely to identify with the working class than were non-unionists (*147*, pp. 28–30). In Britain Blackburn found that among male bank clerks 'the higher a man's perceived social status, the more likely is he to have preferred the staff association to N.U.B.E. [National Union of Bank Employees] or to have joined neither'. But this relationship did not hold among his sample of female bank clerks (*15*, p. 199).

It is impossible to draw any sound conclusions from such a small number of case studies, especially when their findings are somewhat contradictory. It would be difficult enough even if the studies were more plentiful and had more consistent findings. For studies of this nature suffer from methodological and conceptual shortcomings. To begin with, 'there is the well-known problem that phrasing affects response: the researcher gets what he asks for' (*245*, p. 17). The responses vary greatly depending upon whether the questions are of the open-ended or forced-choice variety, and, even where they are of the latter type, the responses vary considerably according to the choices which are offered (*245*, pp. 17–19; *84*, pp. 143–4).

Not only do the questions and choices presented to the respondent affect the nature of the response received, but the responses received are difficult to interpret. Responses which appear to be the same may in fact have very different meanings for the various persons making them. For example, 'middle class', may be defined by the respondent to mean, among other things, those 'in the middle' on certain dimensions such as income or education; those in what are generally regarded to be non-manual occupations; or, more restrictively, those in professional occupations, or those who possess certain specific behaviour patterns. Similarly, 'working class' may be used to mean simply all those who work for a living, excluding only the aristocracy and the rentiers; those who are less skilled and less well-paid; or those who adopt a certain life style. In short, the self-placement method does not elicit the respondent's image of the structure of the social stratification system.

It can only be concluded, as Goldthorpe and Lockwood have, 'that the findings of class identification studies conducted via poll-type questioning are of very little sociological value'. It is 'virtually impossible to interpret such data in any way that would provide reliable indications of respondents' class awareness or class consciousness; the scope for abitrary variation and ambiguity is far too great' (*84*, p. 144). It follows from this that studies which establish correlations between class identifications and union membership must be viewed with some scepticism. Scepticism is also called for because none of these studies have controlled for other variables such as size of firm or employment concentration which might influence people to unionize. Indeed, few of these studies appear to have even considered the possibility that union membership might determine class identification rather than vice versa, or that the two variables might be mutually dependent.

III. CONCLUSION

An analysis of the available evidence concerning the degree of unionization among various groups of workers and a fairly wide range of objective, accorded, and subjective measures or dimensions of their position in the social stratification system has failed to reveal a significant relationship between these two variables. While this casts considerable doubt upon the validity of Hypotheses A and B which posit such a relationship, it does not necessarily 'prove' that they have no substance whatsoever. The data are too sparse and suffer from too many conceptual and methodological shortcomings to allow such a firm conclusion to be drawn. Even if this were not the case, certain possibilities not examined in this chapter would have to be considered before these hypotheses could be completely discounted.

It is possible that results more favourable to these hypotheses might be produced by using other measures of position in the stratification system. For example, it is conceivable that the propensity to unionize is linked to a sense of relative deprivation in terms of social stratification. In other words, the degree to which workers unionize may be determined by the extent to which there is a difference between the position they think they *actually* occupy and the position they think they *should* occupy in the stratification system.

Similarly, although there would seem to be no significant relationship between unionization and any of the dimensions of stratification discussed in this chapter when they are considered separately, it is possible that such a relationship might be found if the effect of some of these dimensions of stratification upon unionization were considered jointly. Individuals and groups may rank high on one dimension of stratification such as education and low on another such as income. Research suggests that such 'stratification inconsistency' produces types of behaviour different from those caused by stratification consistency, with each specific pattern of inconsistency having its own specific consequences (*140*). Hence it is possible that a specific pattern of stratification inconsistency could be significantly related to unionization.

The advocates of Hypotheses A and B have not explicitly considered the possible impact upon unionization of either relative deprivation in terms of stratification or stratification inconsistency. This is probably at least partly because these concepts cannot easily be made operational. It would be difficult to devise an accurate and consistent scale to measure the differences between actual and desired positions in the stratification system. It would be no less difficult to assess the inter-relationships among the various dimensions of stratification and their effect upon unionization, especially when some of these dimensions might themselves be effected by unionization. But even if the difficulties involved in making these concepts operational were overcome, there are reasons for believing that they would not generally be significantly related to unionization.

The decision to join a union is generally not a completely voluntary act, but is, to a greater or lesser extent, constrained by the institutionalization of unions. Kornhauser has made this point very well, and it is worth quoting her at some length:

> When union membership is small and unions newly formed and precariously established, their membership is more likely to be composed of people having especially favorable attitudes toward unions. Union membership will be selective rather than inclusive, and will result from the tendency of workers with similar characteristics to be drawn to unions.... Thus a wider range of social, economic, and political attitudes will be correlated with union membership, and whatever factors engender those attitudes will also be correlated with union membership. ... In short, where union membership is dependent on the self-selection of like-minded individuals, union members will differ substantially from non-members in the attitudes by which members are selected, as well as in the objective characteristics to which the attitudes are related....
>
> But under certain conditions, unions become institutionalized; that is, they are accepted as legitimate participants in industrial rule-making. In these circumstances, union membership ceases to be small and selective; it becomes large and tends indiscriminately to incorporate most individuals in occupations and areas where the jurisdiction of unions has become established. Once a practice is firmly established, its enforcement is no longer dependent on the

voluntary selection of individuals who choose to conform, but rather, conformity tends to become obligatory, either through custom (backed by informal social pressure) or coercion (backed by legal sanctions), both of which presuppose public recognition of the legitimacy of the practice. Consequently, when unions are completely institutionalized, there should be no association between union membership and attitudes formed prior to unionization, for union membership is no longer confined to individuals whose favorable orientations lead them to unions; it now includes many who are indifferent and some who are hostile to unionism, but who join because membership is either customary among their fellows or compulsory for those in their employment situation (*135*, pp. 51–2).

Since unionism has to a considerable extent become institutionalized in most advanced industrial societies, it is now unlikely to be strongly related to the various dimensions of stratification or to the attitudes these engender. Such factors are likely to be linked to unionization, if at all, only during the early stages of its development or in sectors where its institutionalization has not proceeded very far.

But there is still at least one other way in which social stratification might be linked to unionization. Writers such as Blackburn (*15*) have argued that the growth of unions is determined by their character, and that this, in turn, is related to stratification variables. This argument is considered in the following chapter.

3

Social Stratification and Union Character

Social stratification, as Chapter 1 demonstrated, has been linked to union character in a variety of ways. It has been argued that because white-collar and manual workers occupy different positions in the social stratification system, the character of white-collar unionism differs significantly from that of manual unionism. It has also been argued that the most significant difference in social position is that between professional and non-professional workers, with the result that the character of professional unions and associations is quite distinct from the character of both white-collar and manual unions. Finally, it has been suggested that trade unionism is necessarily a class activity and that the character of a union may thus be taken as an index of the class consciousness of its members.

In order to assess the relationship between union character and social stratification, this chapter will attempt to answer three questions. To what extent are white-collar unions different from manual unions? To what extent are professional associations different from trade unions? And to what extent may the character of a union be taken as an index of the class consciousness of its members?

I. WHITE-COLLAR AND MANUAL UNIONS

Many writers have claimed that the character of white-collar unionism differs significantly from that of manual unionism. In advancing this argument, they have generally distinguished between white-collar and manual unions in terms of two major dimensions of character: organizational goals and organizational behaviour.

Organizational Goals

Rawson has argued on the basis of Australian experience that a distinguishing characteristic of manual unions is 'the breadth of their objectives' which include 'aims outside the furtherance of their sectional interests'. In contrast, white-collar unions 'are not concerned with their members as employees, or even as middle-class employees or white-collar employees, but simply as bank clerks, insurance officers or public servants as the case may be'. They are, in other words, concerned merely with the 'grinding of a sectional economic axe' and 'lack any concept of the common interest of all employees' (*187*, pp. 199, 201, 203).

Rawson offered no empirical evidence in support of this argument, but if it were true, as Martin has observed,

> then there would not have been whitecollar union protests against certain features of government budgets in 1964, nor the official support given by the Australian Council of Salaried and Professional Associations and the High Council of Commonwealth Public Service Organisations to proposals for price controls and government action against monopolies, nor the A.C.S.P.A.'s public statements of opinion on such matters as capital gains, income tax policy and foreign capital. Even the close attention which teachers' unions have for many years given government education policies displays a concern with issues which seem to involve much more than simply the promotion of teachers' 'sectional interests'; and, in lesser degree perhaps, the same may be true of the vigorous campaign waged against the old-age pension means test by the New South Wales Public Service Association....

And if most, but by no means all, whitecollar unions do not concern themselves with the grand issues involving war and peace, neither do a great many manual unions (*160*, p. 142).

The general thesis of Martin's rebuttal also holds good for Britain and other countries. In Britain white-collar unions have passed resolutions and pressured governments over issues far removed from their members' narrow sectional interests. There is room to cite only two examples here. The 1956 conference of the Association of Engineering and Shipbuilding Draughtsmen

> carried resolutions reaffirming A.E.S.D. policy on wages, three weeks' holiday and overtime. It decided to discontinue its corporate subscription to the Royal Institute of International Affairs and to affiliate to the Movement for Colonial Freedom. It also instructed the E.C. to permit A.E.S.D. branches to affiliate to local branches of the National Council of Civil Liberties (the Association was already affiliated nationally to the N.C.C.L.). A resolution was adopted on Cyprus criticizing the arrest and deportation of Archbishop Makarios (*171*, pp. 390–1).

During the late 1960s, the Association of Teachers in Technical Institutions and the National Union of Teachers passed resolutions criticising government defence policy and suggesting a re-allocation of resources towards housing and education (*36*, p. 83). As a reading of the conference proceedings of most British white-collar unions will indicate, the draughtsmen and teachers are by no means unique in concerning themselves with issues of wider importance.

The French Federation de l'Education Nationale (F.E.N.) also underlines the inadequacy of Rawson's sharp distinction between the wide goals of manual unions and the narrow goals of white-collar unions. It has adopted policy positions on the 'defense of the Republic, defense of civil liberties and human rights, and defense of the rights of peoples to self-determination and self-government'. In the area of international politics, this major French white-collar union 'supported the strikers in the Berlin riots of June 1953; consistently opposed atomic bomb tests even for France; favored a reduction in the length of military service; [and] favored the admission of Red China to the United Nations as early as 1950'. It was also concerned in the 1950s with pressing successive governments on the need for a negotiated peace in Algeria, and actually took strike action against the granting of special powers to General de Gaulle in 1958. In fact, the F.E.N. took strike action for overtly political ends on seven separate occasions between 1951 and 1962 (*34*, pp. 37–8).

Even granted that manual unions do not have 'broader' objectives than white-collar unions, the two types of unions may nevertheless have different objectives. Writers such as Strauss (*217*, pp. 78–9) and Goldstein (*77*, pp. 203–4) have argued, for example, that white-collar (and professional) unions, unlike their manual counterparts, reject such measures as the closed shop and are opposed to the standardization of working conditions with the result that their collective agreements stress merit rather than seniority as the basis for salary increases and promotions.

Obviously, white-collar and manual unions are sometimes concerned with different kinds of bargaining issues and in some cases even have different policies with respect to the same bargaining issues, if only because of the different job contents and work contexts of their members. But it is very doubtful if the content of collective bargaining provides a suitable basis for polarizing white-collar and manual unions. Walker has noted that 'seniority as applied ... to the opportunity for promotion, has been a favorite objective of the government white-collar unions as of the manual workers' in Australia (*240*, p. 17). Similarly, Swedish white-collar unions 'insist on inclusion in wage systems of seniority and/or "qualification" increments based on length of service' (*173*, p. 290). Even Strauss has conceded that white-collar and manual unions end up in the long-run with similar policies on job evaluation and seniority (*217*, pp. 78–9). In Hartfiel's view, a 'comparison of the charters and the basic programs of the German Trade Union Federation and the German Trade Union for White-Collar Employees does not reveal any important differences' (*102*, p. 151). McCormick has observed that the policies of the British Association of Colliery Management 'on such topics as salaries, superannuation, negotiation machinery and ... recession in the coal industry show little difference from those espoused by' the National Union of Mineworkers (*164*, p. 368). Kassalow has concluded that in the United States

> it is easy to exaggerate the differences between blue-collar and white-collar groups. Once organized, white-collar groups seem to negotiate agreements that show more similarities than differences when compared to manual workers' agreements (*127*, p. 362).

Organizational Behaviour

In documenting the uniqueness of white-collar unions, most attention has been given to their patterns of behaviour. They constitute, in Routh's view, 'an army that shows up well on the parade ground but about whose willingness or ability to shoot there is much doubt' (*195*, p. 201). The same view has been put even more forcefully and fully by Allen:

> white-collar workers establish and extend trade unions ... But the methods they use differ from the traditional union methods because they cannot dispense readily with the values which have led them in the past to denigrate crude industrial action. They are presented with a conflict between what is industrially expedient and that which is socially permissible. They employ collective bargaining

and arbitration more frequently than manual workers as their sole means of protection.... With few exceptions white-collar unions try to avoid political party alignments. Their members are conservative by conditioning, preferring to conform and be safe (*4*, p. 173).

Rawson has also distinguished white-collar and manual unions in terms of the willingness of the latter and the reluctance of the former to enter into common affiliation with other employee organizations and with political parties (*187*, pp. 196–8).

But there is a considerable body of evidence which suggests that it is not possible to polarize white-collar and manual unions in terms of their behaviour patterns. Participation in strikes and other forms of militant action, as well as affiliation to other employee organizations and political parties, is no monopoly of manual unions. The Central Organization of Swedish Professional Workers, S.A.C.O., ran a teachers' strike in 1966 and called out civil servants in a three-day sympathy action (*128*, pp. 130–2). White-collar unions in Japan, particularly those in the public sector, are very militant, 'and it is through the government unions that the major labor center, *Sōhyō*, conducts most of its political and economic campaigns (*143*, p. 114).

In France, Clark has documented the political and industrial militancy of the teachers (*34*), and Reynaud has noted the part played by the 'cadre' (managers and technicians) in some of the strike movements of the last ten years and their affiliation to the main federations of manual workers' unions (*189*, p. 153). Crozier has also pointed out that French white-collar unions 'are in the main stream of the French labor movement'. They have 'patterns of action in many ways similar to those of other French unions', and, in particular, 'have struck quite often' (*43*, pp. 111, 120, 125).

Australian white-collar unions 'have displayed increasing interest in direct industrial action', 'have become less diffident on the subject of political action', and have increasingly emphasised 'the value of common action for common ends (*161*, pp. 20–1). And as Martin has further noted in refuting Rawson's contention that only manual unions have affiliated to labour federations or to political parties in Australia, 'common affiliations of one kind or another are possessed by almost half of the whitecollar unions in Australia, and these 92 affiliated unions account for the great bulk of whitecollar unionists' (*160*, p. 135). Moreover, 'there are at least 22 separate whitecollar unions affiliated to one, or more in the case of interstate unions, of the state branches of the Australian Labor Party' (p. 140).

A similar situation exists in Britain. Writing in 1961, Allen pointed out that

> Recently ... we have witnessed the spectacle of school-teachers going on strike; of solicitors working to rule; of scientists parading their grievances through the streets of London; of insurance men lobbying the House of Lords; of chemists threatening to leave the National Health Service; of a vicar suggesting a trade union for clergymen.
>
> .   .   .
>
> Nor is it the first time they have used militant methods. All were particularly aggressive after the first world war. There were strikes among bank clerks in Ireland, insurance agents in Scotland, and school teachers in England and Wales. Various other groups threatened strike action. Civil Servants demonstrated in their masses against the Government.
>
> Since the second world war a number of industrial protests have been made. In 1950 doctors decided to leave the National Health Service, but afterwards changed their minds, and in 1957 health-service workers imposed a ban on overtime; on various occasions clerks in the motor industry have gone on strike (*3*, p. 895).

Since Allen wrote, there have been further strikes of

teachers, bank clerks, draughtsmen, industrial clerks, and airline pilots, to mention only a few white-collar groups.

Many white-collar unions in Britain have also affiliated to the Trades Union Congress and the Labour Party. Forty-four of the 229 purely white-collar unions and all of the 19 partially white-collar unions operating in the United Kingdom in 1970 were affiliated to the T.U.C., and they accounted for 78 per cent of total white-collar union membership (*8*, pp. 24–5). Nine of the purely white-collar unions and 18 of the partially white-collar unions were also affiliated to the Labour Party in 1970, and they accounted for 34 per cent of total white-collar union membership. Indeed, such white-collar unions as the Association of Scientific, Technical and Managerial Staffs, the Association of Cinematograph, Television and Allied Technicians, and the Draughtsmen's and Allied Technicians' Association emerged as major critics of what they perceived as the Labour Government's right-wing policies after 1964.

Manual and white-collar unions cannot be polarized in terms of their behaviour patterns not only because many white-collar unions have engaged in militant action and common affiliations, but also because many manual unions have not. For example, the General Secretary of the major association of manual workers in the British steel industry, the Iron and Steel Trades Confederation, summarized his union's record as follows:

> Since its formation the Confederation has a record of responsible conduct which speaks for itself. There has been no official strike involving our members since the General Strike of 1926 ... The reason for this is that the Confederation believes in conducting its affairs in a responsible and intelligent way. It does not regard itself as one of two sides ranged against each other in a state of permanent hostility, but as part of a joint enterprise which reconciles its problems against a background of

common interest ... The fact that there has been no
serious strike of Confederation members in the industry
for a great number of years is evidence of the harmonious
relations which exist between the employers and the Confederation (*94*, p. 30).

Ironically, this statement was made in defence of the
Confederation's claim to negotiating rights for white-
collar workers in the steel industry, and in opposition to
the encroachment of more militant white-collar unions.

Although the vast bulk of manual union membership
in Britain is affiliated to the T.U.C., there are numerous
minor manual unions which remain unaffiliated. Even
more manual unions have not affiliated to the Labour
Party. And they include, as Harrison has pointed out,
'such undoubtedly working-class unions as the National
Amalgamated Stevedores and Dockers, United Road
Transport Workers' Association, Amalgamated Society
of Wire Drawers and Kindred Workers, Scottish Typographical Association, Iron, Steel and Metal Dressers'
Trade Society, National Union of Hosiery Workers,
Amalgamated Society of Leather Workers, and Amalgamated Society of Lithographic Printers'. Indeed, by
showing that 'the lessons of trade union experience' do
not 'point irrevocably to affiliation with the Labour
Party this group of unions is a standing challenge to one
of the Movement's most cherished myths' (*101*, pp. 325,
334).

Conclusion

The above evidence leads to the conclusion that the characters of white-collar and manual unions are not fundamentally dissimilar. Other writers have come to much
the same conclusion. Blackburn and Prandy have suggested that it is 'most fruitful to place emphasis on the
basic similarity of white-collar to other unions' (*16*, p.
120). Lockwood has claimed that 'generally speaking the

overall tendency has been for blackcoated workers to form associations fashioned after those of working-class trade unions' (*150*, pp. 194–5). And Mills has argued that

> The psychology of white-collar unionism ... is not different from that of wage-workers; ... Of course, unions of carpenters differ in shape and policy from unions of auto workers or insurance salesmen or clerks. But the common denominators of unionism are not divided according to white-collar and wage-worker types.

.   .   .

> The lesson from the historical experience of unionism in the United States ... is that wage-workers and white-collar employees in due course form the same types of unions, and that there is nothing peculiar or distinctive about white-collar unionism; that variations in terms of militancy among wage-worker unions and among white-collar unions are just as slight as any other variations between the two. (*170*, pp. 316–18).

The distinction between white-collar and manual unions is, as Martin has pointed out, 'at least deceptive and probably valueless if the aim is to classify trade unions in terms of the way they behave'. This is because it is based on two dubious assumptions. First, that the two groups of unions can be differentiated by behavioural characteristics exclusive to each; second, that there are no significant differences in the behaviour of unions within any one group. Neither assumption is valid. 'Such empirical evidence as is available points, instead, to a spectrum of behaviour on which there is a substantial overlap between the two categories of unions' (*160*, p. 143.)

In short, to polarize white-collar and manual unions into two distinct types is to engage in caricature. Manual unions are seen as bargaining over primarily economic matters and demonstrating acute propensities for industrial and political militancy. White-collar unions, on the other hand, are presented as being concerned primarily with their members' social status and as being industrially and politically conservative. The distinction is too crude. All that can safely be said is that, historically, certain forms of industrial and political action have been more common among manual unions. But they have never been totally prevalent among such unions, or totally absent from white-collar unions; and the evidence suggests that the differences in patterns of behaviour within the white-collar and manual union categories are at least as great as the differences between them. Thus the distinction between the two types of unions is, at most, one of degree, not one of kind.

Some writers accept this conclusion but nevertheless argue that these differences of degree in union character are explained by stratification variables. Lockwood, for example, has suggested that differences in the characters of unions are caused by differences in their members' social origins and status, work situations, and, in particular, economic positions. In his view, 'the character of blackcoated unionism, no less than its extent, is an outcome of the class situation of the clerk, and variations in the former are to be understood in terms of variations in the latter' (*150*, p. 198).

Lockwood offers very little evidence to substantiate his claim, and its validity is doubtful. Taking some of the dimensions of character which Lockwood himself specifies, it can be seen that groups with similar social positions form unions with different characters. English printers are affiliated to the Labour Party but Scottish printers in the Scottish Typographical Association are not. The National Union of Teachers is affiliated to the T.U.C., but the National Association of Head Teachers is not, even though 80 per cent of its members also belong to the N.U.T. Both the National Union of Bank Employees and various staff associations recruit bank clerks, but only N.U.B.E. has affiliated to the T.U.C. or engaged in strike action.

Similarly, unions whose members occupy different social positions have many similar aspects to their characters. The Association of Scientific, Technical and Managerial Staffs and the Association of Professional, Executive, and Computer Staffs are affiliated to the T.U.C. and the Labour Party as are the National Union of Mineworkers and the Amalgamated Union of Engineering Workers. Indeed, the very fact that many, if not most, unions in Britain recruit members from relatively heterogeneous social groupings, often including both white-collar and manual workers, suggests that there is no simple relationship between a union's character and the social position of its membership.

Finally, if union characters are determined by their members' social positions, then how can the former change while the latter remains the same? There were no significant changes in the social positions of the members of the National and Local Government Officers Association or the National Association of Schoolmasters during the 1960s, yet both of them reversed long standing positions and affiliated to the T.U.C. And if social position determines union character, then how can a single individual hold dual membership in two organizations with different characters as is the case among some clerical workers in banking and among some professionals in engineering? Clearly, the relationship between union character and social position is far more complex and tenuous than Lockwood's argument suggests.

II. PROFESSIONAL ASSOCIATIONS AND TRADE UNIONS

Several writers have suggested that the social cleavage between professionals and non-professionals is more significant than that between white-collar and manual workers, and they have drawn a sharp distinction between associations of professional workers and unions of white-collar and manual workers. The distinction has been drawn in terms of the same two dimensions of character: organizational goals and organizational behaviour.

Organizational Goals

Those early students of professionalism, Carr-Saunders and Wilson, argued that the goals of professional associations and trade unions differ significantly. 'The trade union is virtually a single-purpose association' in which 'the protective function overshadows all others in importance'. Although 'the protective motive is present' among professional associations, 'it is only one among many and by no means always the most important'. In their view, a more important goal of professional associations is 'to hall-mark the competent and to foster the study of the technique' (32, p. 319). The views of Carr-Saunders and Wilson have prevailed, and professional associations are still generally presented as being primarily interested in such goals as increasing the status of the profession, promoting the study of specific subjects, qualifying the competent, and thereby serving and protecting the public. Trade unions, on the other hand, are commonly portrayed as being almost solely interested in promoting the economic interests of their members.

In assessing this argument it is necessary to distinguish between various types of professional bodies. Millerson has classified them into four categories. First, there are Prestige Associations such as the Royal Society and the British Academy, membership of which is generally regarded as conferring special prestige. Second, there are Study Associations such as the Royal Statistical Society and the British Sociological Association which attempt to study and promote a specific subject. Third, there are Qualifying Associations such as the Royal Institute of British Architects and the Law Society which aim at qualifying by examination those who wish to practice in a subject. Finally, there are the Occupational Associations which Millerson sub-divides into Co-ordinating Associations such as the Society of County Treasurers and Protective Associations such as the British Medical Association. The former tries to improve the working conditions and remuneration of members by co-ordinating their professional activities but without extensive negotiations or the application of pressure techniques. The latter 'provides an organized means of exercising pressure to protect and improve the working conditions and remuneration of the individual professional' (*168*, pp. 26–41).

Millerson's typology might be criticised in certain respects, but it nevertheless provides a useful classification for the purpose of this discussion. Inasmuch as the above description of professional association goals is meant to apply to prestige and study associations, it is largely accurate for they do not generally attempt to regulate the jobs of their members. But inasmuch as it is meant to apply to qualifying and occupational associations, it is oversimplified and misleading. For the concern of these associations with study, qualifications, and public service has always been closely linked with their concern to control the supply of professional labour and to increase the incomes of their members.

Although it is not usual for qualifying associations to engage directly in negotiations on salaries and conditions, as Blackburn has pointed out,

> their activities may have considerable influence in this field. Most directly, control over the numbers gaining a desired qualification means control of the market, which is of prime importance in determining pay and conditions.... Other protective tactics which may be adopted include: (a) remuneration surveys among members; (b) advice to individual members on terms of contracts and suitability of salaries; (c) advice and information on con-

tracts and salaries (to employers); (d) use of an appointments register or the journal to inform members of vacancies; (e) warnings to members against taking up particular appointments; (f) support in the formation of a new body to conduct negotiations (*15*, pp. 24–5).

Indeed, Millerson's survey of the codes of qualifying associations demonstrated that these bodies 'show greatest concern over competition: firstly, in terms of finding work; secondly, with the method of payment', and that there was 'very little emphasis ... on service to clients, or on any duty to expose professional incompetence' (*168*, p. 165).

Job regulation is an even more important part of the activities of occupational associations. The protective association, in particular, as Blackburn has again noted, is

> usually prepared to participate in direct negotiations and bargaining over salaries and conditions ... But regardless of whether it bargains or not, ... its sole major function is the protection of the occupational interests of the members, whatever means it may use.
>
> .   .   .
>
> Thus, in this respect, the characters of professional associations occupy the full range up to the level where it is rather arbitrary whether we choose to call them protective associations or trade unions (*15*, pp. 25–7).

Lipset has made a similar point:

> In acquiring the mandate to say who can and cannot practice, the association protects its members who have fulfilled the formally prescribed training from the untrained amateurs, popularly known as quacks who claim the same occupational status. This struggle for status has also been part of a fight for higher income, and thus is in a real sense related to conventional trade union objectives (*147*, p. 63).

Perhaps not surprisingly, therefore, Kleingartner

found nothing in 'the history of the independent professions or in the activities of their associations to suggest that professions must exercise self-denial in matters of economics and work control' (*131*, p. 106). In fact, what professionals term 'professional control' in their own associations, they often denigrate as 'restrictive practices' in trade unions. The Engineers' Guild, for example, claimed that

> The 'closed shop' idea in certain artisan trades is adopted largely to prevent unemployment of skilled union members. The object of the Guild is to restrict employment on professional engineering work to those persons who are fully qualified, practically and theoretically, not merely for the benefit of engineers only, but for the ultimate advantage of the general public whose safety often depends on competent engineering work (cited by *164*, p. 367).

Although the Engineers' Guild seemed to be unaware of it, most unions of skilled workers would employ the same argument in justifying their demands for a closed shop. In any case, even if the reasons differ, as McCormick has pointed out, 'licensing of practitioners of a particular kind of activity and the refusal to reduce fees are aspects of a good code of ethics, but they are not unrelated to economic standards' (p. 367). Similarly, Eckstein has observed of the British Medical Association that it

> has never been able to fight down its trade union impulse; indeed a great many of the public-spirited activities on which it now prides its conscience were more concerned with the bread-and-butter interests of the doctors than the medical needs of the public (*58*, p. 347).

In short, 'professional' and 'economic' objectives are often intertwined, and to allot the first to professional associations and the second to trade unions is to be misled by different formulations of basically similar preoccupations.

Organizational Behaviour

Even granted that professional associations* and trade unions share the same basic goal—to influence the rules under which their members work—it is often suggested that they use different methods to achieve this goal. Kleingartner has argued that although some professional associations adopt the methods of unions, 'in structure and in style they are quite separate from established unions': unions use 'bargaining power' while professional associations tend to rely on 'internal improvement or public acceptance' (*132*, p. 84; *131*, p. 55). Millerson has claimed that even when professional associations participate in collective bargaining, 'they dislike resorting to the drastic action methods of trade unions' (*168*, p. 14).† He sees the 'true trade union tactics' as 'strikes, working to rule, compulsory membership, [and] demarcation disputes' (p. 41).

Professionals and their associations may dislike trade

* Unless otherwise noted, the term 'professional association', is henceforth used in this study to refer only to Qualifying and Occupational Associations and not to Prestige or Study Associations.

† Millerson has also claimed that in addition to the professional associations' dislike of trade union tactics, the two types of organizations differ in several other respects. Professional associations, unlike trade unions, are of many types, multi-functional, generally incorporated, often have more than one membership grade indicating degrees of competence, contain employers and self-employed as well as employees, and rarely have compulsory membership. But even the most cursory survey of trade unions indicates that they also possess most of these characteristics. They are of many types—craft, industrial, general, closed, and open; are multi-functional—economic, social, and political; and have, at least in the case of craft unions, more than one membership grade indicating different levels of competence. Moreover, some unions such as the National Federation of Sub-Postmasters are composed entirely of self-employed persons. While it is true that unions are not incorporated under the Companies Acts or by Royal Charter, it is doubtful if this difference is of much sociological significance. And it would take considerably more evidence than Millerson offers to prove his debatable claim that joining a professional association is a more 'voluntary' process than joining a trade union.

union tactics, but they nevertheless use them. Kassalow has written of 'strikes or serious strike threats in recent years by doctors in Belgium, Canada, Great Britain, and Israel; nurses in the U.S., Britain, and Sweden; teachers in the U.S., Canada, Sweden, Britain, and France; and engineers in the U.S. and Australia' (*128*, p. 119). Airline pilots 'have shown that they can keep and use the strike effectively, maintain almost one hundred percent membership, and gain stature as a profession' (*131*, pp. 54–5). Similarly, the Belgian doctors strike of 1964 demonstrated that a

> long tradition of professionalism; an environment of economic independence and individualism; and, one might add, the shade of Hippocrates, need not inhibit the rapid development of militant strike-prone unionism (*42*, p. 30).

Practically all of Israel's professionals belong to organizations which, according to Ben-David, 'bargain collectively and use strikes to advance their economic interests'. In fact, 'strikes have become as much part of the routine of collective bargaining of the professionals in Israel as of auto workers in America' (*14*, pp. 61, 59). Sweden provides the ultimate example: the Union of Swedish Church Clergymen which although it did not participate in the Central Organization of Swedish Professional Workers (S.A.C.O.) strike of 1966, did contribute to the parent organization's conflict fund (*128*, p. 125).

Conclusion

Trade unions and professional associations are both concerned with job regulation: each tries to shape the rules under which its members work. While it is true that many professional associations use unilateral regulation rather than collective bargaining to establish and administer the rules which govern their members on the job, this does not make them qualitatively different from trade unions. For many unions rely upon unilateral regulation to defend such practices as job demarcation and apprentice/journeyman ratios, and, historically, craft unions even succeeded in regulating wages and other terms and conditions of employment unilaterally.*

In fact, rather than being distinct from trade unions, professional associations can more accurately be portrayed as the craft unions of a different social group. The craft union of manual workers

> sought to reserve to its members the exclusive right to perform all jobs which knowledge of their craft enabled them to perform. This implied the exclusion of non-craftsmen, or 'specialists', as well as the inclusion of all relevant jobs within the jurisdiction ... Less frequently, it sought actively to enlarge this sphere of opportunity by holding down the number of qualified craftsmen through restrictive apprenticeship regulations, but the relatively less frequent occurrence of this type of regulation was due primarily to lack of opportunity rather than to any inherent reluctance to restrict numbers (*235*, p. 579).

Similarly, 'the first aim of the typical professional organization', as Prandy has pointed out, is 'to secure control over entrance to the occupation, and then to control minimum, and sometimes maximum fees'. As with the successful craft union, the effect of this creation of a 'closed shop' by the professional association is to give its members 'monopoly control of the market' (*185*, pp 67–8).

The distinction between professional associations and trade unions, like that between white-collar and manual unions, is at most one of degree, not one of kind. As Reynaud has pointed out,

> Perhaps because in French the same word—*syndicat*—is

---

* See *infra*, pp. 87–9, for a fuller discussion of this point.

used to describe the associations of doctors, of employees and of employers alike, it seems to us that there are only differences of degree between these organisations, as between the methods they adopt. In brief, professionalisation, over and above its marked affinities with traditional craft unionism, seems to us to represent one possible orientation of union action rather than an alternative possibility to such action (*189*, p. 155).

Even Prandy who is at some pains to maintain the distinction between professional associations and trade unions, is forced to conclude that although unions among professional workers are different from those among manual workers,

the similarities are nevertheless greater than the differences. The latter are explained by the different employment situation in which scientists and engineers are placed, and it is highly debatable, in view of the way in which employment situation can change, whether this form of trade unionism is significantly different from others. Trade unionism differs even amongst manual workers ... The existence of unionism amongst this group [professionals] is of greater significance than are the present differences with 'traditional' trade unionism (*184*, p. 145).

This is not to deny that the incidence of certain forms of collective action is generally lower among groups normally defined as professional than among those who are not. Nor is it to deny that the specific policies adopted by professional associations and trade unions often diverge. But the evidence on the similarities in the behaviour of professional associations and trade unions with respect to job regulation indicates that collective action and professional status are not mutually exclusive and that, in consequence, the line drawn between associations of professional and non-professional workers is in practice of very little relevance to the differentiation of distinct character types.

III. UNION CHARACTER AND CLASS CONSCIOUSNESS

The Argument

The preceding analysis has cast considerable doubt upon any simple equation of social stratification and the character of employee organizations. In spite of the different social positions of the members of manual unions, white-collar unions, and professional associations, differences in the character of these organizations are more those of degree than of kind: for character differences within each organizational category are at least as great as those between each category. Even these differences of degree in the character of employee organizations do not seem to be determined by the differences in their members' social positions. But there is still another way in which social stratification has been linked to union character. Certain writers have argued that a union's character is an index of the class consciousness of its members.

For Lockwood 'the trade-union movement is a working-class movement, and to the extent that clerical workers become involved in trade unionism they have to come to terms with its wider class character' (*150*, p. 137). He assumes that the 'class-conscious feeling of the blackcoated worker is reflected in the degree to which his union identifies itself with the Labour Movement' (p. 197). He suggests that

> Although there can be no accurate measurement of the class consciousness of blackcoated unionism, it can be traced in a variety of indirect ways: by a change in the name and purposes of a clerical association, as when a friendly society is transformed into a genuine trade union; by the adoption and use of certain types of sanctions, such as strike action, for the attainment of its goals; by the affiliation of the association to the wider trade-union movement; by its identification with the political wing of the Labour Movement; by sympathetic behaviour in

critical 'class' situations, such as the General Strike; as well as by the general social and political outlook of the membership and leaders of the association (pp. 137–8).

In short, by assessing the performance of clerical unions against a number of *'general problems'* faced by every union 'by virtue of its status as a defensive organization of employee interests', Lockwood gauges their character and hence the class consciousness of their members (p. 155).

Blackburn has offered a similar but distinctive analysis. 'Unionisation' for him 'is the measure of the social significance of unionism', an 'index of class consciousness' (*15*, pp. 14, 9). He defines unionization as consisting of two variables: union membership and union character. Union membership is measured by 'completeness' or density, the proportion of potential members of a union who are actual members. Union character is measured by what Blackburn calls 'unionateness'. Character can be 'more or less unionate' according to the extent to which the organization 'is a whole-hearted trade union, identifying with the Labour Movement and willing to use all the powers of the Movement'. That is, 'the level of unionateness depends on the commitment of an organisation to the general principles and ideology of trade unionism' (p. 18).

In other words, unionization, the measure of class consciousness, is a function of unionateness and completeness, and within certain specified limits, 'by far the simplest satisfactory formula is *unionisation = unionateness × completeness*' (p. 44). Although Blackburn's formula for unionization 'is symmetrical in its two elements' (p. 270), there is little doubt that he considers unionateness and the union character which it measures to be the primary indicator of class consciousness. This is made clear not only implicitly by the title of his book—*Union Character and Social Class*—and by its contents (pp.

270–1) but also explicitly by the latest formulation of the argument which refers to unionateness 'as a measure of potential for class action' (*17*, p. 88).

Completeness is relatively easy to measure; it is by its very nature a quantitative concept. Unionateness is more difficult to measure. But, in Blackburn's view, 'a useful rough measure' is obtained by considering the extent to which the following seven characteristics apply to an organization:

1. It regards collective bargaining and the protection of the interests of members, as employees, as its main function.
2. It is independent of employers for purposes of negotiation.
3. It is prepared to be militant, 'using all forms of industrial action which may be effective'.
4. It declares itself to be a trade union.
5. It is registered as a trade union.
6. It is affiliated to the Trades Union Congress.
7. It is affiliated to the Labour Party.

These seven elements are very close to those formulated earlier by Lockwood. The first three measure the organization's degree of willingness to use the methods of unions which Blackburn takes to be independent collective bargaining and strike action. The last four measure the degree to which an employee organization is willing to identify openly with other unions, by, for example, joining the same kind of associations such as the Trades Union Congress and the Labour Party.*

---

* The seven criteria are quoted here in the order given by Blackburn (*15*, pp. 18–19). These criteria are also given in Blackburn and Prandy (*16*, p. 112). The latter statement of the argument reverses the order of the criteria, giving items 4 to 7 before items 1 to 3. This suggests that Blackburn is offering a two dimensional measure of character, with unionateness in relation to the employment situation, and unionateness in relation to the wider society. That this is so can be seen in the tentative paper by Blackburn and his colleagues (*17*, pp. 87–92).

An Assessment

This argument undoubtedly makes a significant contribution to the discussion of union character, but serious
problems remain with its use of character as an index
of class consciousness. For 'unionisation' to provide an
adequate index of class consciousness, character as measured by unionateness must isolate a form of behaviour
which is solely, or at least primarily, motivated by a
consciousness of class ties. In other words, an organization's score on any of the seven dimensions of
unionateness is only significant, within the context of
Blackburn's and Lockwood's argument, inasmuch as
the motivation for taking the action which is being
measured derives from a feeling of solidarity with the
wider working class as opposed to the narrowly conceived needs of the organization itself or the sectional
economic needs of its members. Hence in assessing the
above argument it is necessary to determine to what
extent the seven dimensions of unionateness indicate a
sense of class solidarity as opposed merely to recording
responses to narrow sectional needs and interests. It will
facilitate the discussion of these seven dimensions if they
are grouped as follows: declaration and registration as
a union, independent collective bargaining, militancy,
and affiliation to the Trades Union Congress and the
Labour Party.

Declaration and registration as a union. Whether or
not an organization calls itself a trade union, or registers
as such, may indicate something about the class consciousness of its members. But equally it may not. A
union's reluctance to declare itself as such may stem
not from a lack of class consciousness on the part of
its present membership, but from an assumed lack of
consciousness on the part of a potential membership
which it is attempting to recruit. Moreover, a union may

not openly declare itself in an attempt to have a stronger appeal for employers and thereby more easily obtain recognition from them. Similarly, there may be legal and other disadvantages imposed on unions by the state, and they may not wish to identify themselves as such in an attempt to escape these.

Similarly, registration* is a poor measure of class consciousness primarily because unions often base their decision on factors which are unconnected with any sense of class solidarity they may possess. There are certain legal and administrative advantages to registration (*92*, pp. 47–8), and many unions register because of these. For example, the Association of Scientific Workers decided to register following the discovery of 'its weak legal position in negotiating a particular issue' (*184*, p. 137). Hence, as Prandy has observed, 'Even where an organization has taken advantage of the legal benefits of registration this is no indication that it thereby recognizes itself as a body similar to other trade unions, especially those of manual workers' (p. 141). Moreover, structural factors have sometimes prevented an organization which would like to register from doing so. The British Medical Association took legal advice in 1910 'as to whether it could register as a trade union: the ruling was negative, since it was an association neither of workmen nor masters' (*195*, p. 175). Hence, as Blackburn himself concludes, 'we should not ... pay too much heed to the legal status of an organisation' as an indicator of its 'sociological character' (*15*, p. 37).

* Blackburn advanced his argument prior to the passage of the Industrial Relations Act 1971 which has changed the nature of union registration. Hence his argument is assessed in relation to the situation prevailing prior to the passage of the Act. Paradoxically, it might now be argued that a class conscious union would refuse to register since this has been the central plank in the Trades Union Congress' strategy in opposing the Industrial Relations Act. But it would be unwise to draw even this conclusion without first examining in detail the extent to which such organizational needs as growth or legal protection influence a union's decision to register.

Even granted for the moment that an organization's decision to register or declare itself as a union could indicate something significant about the class consciousness of its members, it is difficult to see how these dimensions of unionateness can be operationalized. Blackburn takes a union's decision to register as such under the law as a dimension of unionateness because 'registration implies that an organisation acknowledges its role as a trade union, with the same functions as other unions and so part of the trade-union movement' (p. 36). While this may sometimes be the case, it is not always so. The Union of Post Office Workers in Britain and the Waterside Workers' Federation in New South Wales have never registered as trade unions, but there is little doubt that they consider themselves as such. Other organizations are registered but clearly do not see themselves as unions. The United Kingdom Association of Professional Engineers was created by members of the Engineers' Guild specifically to prevent 'infiltration' among engineers by white-collar trade unions. Although 'it will be registered as a trade union', as its treasurer pointed out, 'it will not behave like one' (*The Times*, 13 January 1969). And although eighty-one employers' associations were registered as trade unions in Britain in 1966 (*95*, p. 210), they obviously did not consider themselves as such and registration hardly measured their members' consciousness of solidarity with working class goals, institutions, or traditions.

Similarly, as Blackburn himself has pointed out, 'it is not easy to decide whether an organisation does or does not declare itself to be a trade union' (*15*, p. 36). He originally suggested that an organization's title was a useful indicator in this regard; if it wanted to avoid declaring itself as a union, it would use such words as 'association' or 'guild' (*16*, pp. 112–13). But surely the Association of Supervisory, Technical and Managerial Staffs, the National Graphical Association, and the

British Iron and Steel and Kindred Trades Association have declared themselves to be unions no less than have the Union of Shop, Distributive and Allied Workers, the National Union of Bank Employees, and the National Union of Teachers. In fact, less than 50 per cent of the unions affiliated to the Trades Union Congress in 1970 had the word 'union' in their title. This is hardly surprising for, as Commons has pointed out, 'the original word for a union of wage-earners was "society" or "association"', and it was not until the 1830s 'that the term "trade union" came into vogue, both in England and the United States' (*38*, pp. 14–15; see also *242*, pp. 113–14).

Blackburn himself has subsequently suggested in a more recent statement of his argument that an organization's title is not a reliable indicator of unionateness. In his words,

> the title is of limited utility as an indicator of character, if only because titles were usually adopted many years ago and have not changed with changes in character. Thus the words used in the name of an organisation may be misleading. It is possible that the titles of the N.U.T. [National Union of Teachers] and C.S.C.A. [Civil Service Clerical Association] contributed to the confusion concerning these bodies ... At any rate these two organisations provide an illustration of the unreliability of titles in indicating the public image an organisation wishes to create. It is true that if an organisation is sufficiently concerned it can change its name, but there are always good reasons for not doing so (*15*, p. 36).

He goes on to consider if the opinions of members can serve as a useful guide as to whether or not an organization declares itself to be a trade union, but he suggests that they do not as the members 'may not all be in agreement with, or even aware of official attitudes'. He concludes that 'the deciding factor is the official view of the public image the organisation wants, as expressed in statements and actions' (p. 36). But why are the attitudes of union officials to be preferred to those of union members, especially when it is the latter's class consciousness which the declaration is supposed to measure? And since unions are not monolithic entities, which officials' attitudes, expressed in which statements and actions, and designed for which public's consumption are to be considered most important in this regard? Clearly, there can be no unequivocal answers to these questions, and it can only be concluded that official attitudes are no more a reliable indicator of character than is the title of an organization.

Independent collective bargaining. Independence from employers and collective bargaining are so closely related that it is easiest to consider them together. Blackburn argues that collective bargaining 'is basic to the concept of unionateness'. 'If an organisation has no score under this item, it has no score under the other items, i.e. its level of unionateness is zero' (p. 28). Indeed, he calls collective bargaining and the protection of the interests of members as employees, 'the definitive functions of trade unions' (p. 21).

Blackburn's emphasis upon collective bargaining is somewhat surprising for at least two reasons. To begin with, it conflicts somewhat with his stress on independence from employers. For collective bargaining by its very nature involves mutual dependence. In fact, the more institutionalized the collective bargaining relationship, the greater the mutual dependence. Union and management officials not only accept each other's existence but support certain of each other's objectives. For its part, management supports the strength and stability of the union, allows it to take credit for improvements in wages and working conditions, and does not compete with it for employee loyalty. Paradoxically, there is often more dependence upon management where unions are strong and more unionate (in terms of the other six criteria) than where they are weak and less unionate.

Indeed, some of the weakest and least unionate unions on Blackburn's criteria enjoy the ultimate independence of not even being recognized by employers.

Moreover, regardless of the strength of the union, its degree of independence from employers is rarely indicative of the class consciousness of its members. For independence from employers is generally determined not so much by membership attitudes as by employer policies. The company-dominated unions established in the United States in the 1920s and 1930s, for example, were more revealing of employer than employee aspirations. Even when unions are not dominated by employers, the latter have generally been more successful than the former in shaping the nature of the relationship between them. As Marsh has noted,

> it is historically true that trade union organization, however much the unions may desire change, has rarely acted as a dynamic force in shaping the structure of any industrial relations system.... In the past they have succeeded in forcing negotiations upon employers, but they have very rarely been able to dictate how and at what level and within what framework such negotiations should take place (*157*, p. 217).

The employers have generally been in a position to do this. While it is true that employer policies may be influenced by membership attitudes, these need not necessarily be characterized by class consciousness as the following discussion of militancy makes clear. And whether membership attitudes are class conscious or not, they have often been less important in determining the nature and degree of recognition which employers are prepared to concede to unions than such other factors as government policies, industrial structure, the nature of competition in labour and product markets, and the employer's own ideology.

It is also difficult to see why Blackburn assigns primacy to collective bargaining if the objective is to measure unionateness. For organizations which engage in unilateral regulation have as good, if not better, claim to being committed 'to the general principles and ideology of trade unionism' as organizations which engage in collective bargaining. The early craft unions in Britain and other countries tended to rely almost exclusively upon unilateral regulation. 'Even though the nineteenth-century craft unions achieved only a partial success in their attempt at independent control of their trades', as H. A. Turner has pointed out, 'their whole tradition so predisposed them to the method of autonomous [unilateral] regulation that they made little positive attempt to explore the alternative techniques' (*234*, p. 204).

The reason for this is not hard to find. Craftsmen should regulate 'what we alone have a right to regulate, the value of our labour', as the London Society of Compositors put it in the 1830s, because 'those ... who argue that our employers ought to have been consulted, do not see the extent to which the argument may be applied, for ... it will ultimately lead us into the argument that the masters have the right to regulate [piece] prices' (*35*, p. 5). In short, given that the various methods of job regulation can be equally effective, unions will naturally prefer that method which minimizes the necessity of compromising with external interests. They thus prefer unilateral regulation to collective bargaining which involves compromise and power-sharing. Indeed, such class conscious trade unionists as the syndicalists rejected collective bargaining on principle because this compromise and power-sharing seemed to them the essence of class collaboration. They preferred unions to impose their terms unilaterally upon employers and thereby avoid the risk of contamination by capitalists. Thus, if anything, unilateral regulation could be taken to be more unionate than collective bargaining.

But it does not necessarily follow that unilateral regulation is any better a measure of class consciousness than collective bargaining. For the method of job regulation adopted by unions is determined not so much by the attitudes of their members as by structural factors external to them. Perhaps the key factors in this regard are employer policies and the extent to which unions can control labour supply. Both of these, in turn, have been crucially dependent upon the nature of the trade or industry. For example, rapid technological change in the engineering industry towards the end of the nineteenth century made it increasingly difficult for unions to maintain their craft controls and increasingly expensive for employers to tolerate them. Consequently, the employers banded together and locked the unions out for thirty weeks. As Clegg, Fox, and Thompson point out,

> The employers' ideal, no doubt, was complete managerial freedom. Where this could not be had, they strove for an agreement which would not only establish a means of securing orderly changes in wages and conditions of work as they were required but would also ban the more objectionable restrictive practices (35, p. 169).

In short, the creation of a system of collective bargaining was a function of union weakness rather than strength, and it had little, if anything, to do with the class consciousness of union members.

To summarize, there is more than the one trade union method that Blackburn seems to assume. Moreover, the method which a union chooses is not only or even primarily determined by the class consciousness of its members. Rather, union methods vary with bargaining contexts, and these 'vary so much that the methods which may be appropriate in one situation may be completely inappropriate in another' (5, p. 19). In short, the equation of collective bargaining with trade unionism is false.

Militancy. Blackburn defines militancy as 'the extent to which an organisation will go in asserting the interests of its members against employers—in fulfilling a trade-union function' (*15*, p. 31). In his view the strike is the ultimate in militant behaviour.

The strike is undoubtedly an example of militant behaviour, but it and other forms of militant action need not necessarily be an indicator of class consciousness. Strikes can very often be for sectarian ends and contribute nothing to wider class or even union goals. For example, a strike by white workers against the employment of 'immigrants' in skilled jobs is hardly an example of class solidarity. Neither is a strike of one union against another as a result of a demarcation dispute. In the ship-building industry, as Brown and Brannen point out, 'many of the issues about which there are disputes arise directly from the fact that the occupational groups have separate and often conflicting interests rather than from any overall sense of solidarity' (*24*, p. 206). Hence before any judgement can be given regarding the social significance of a strike, its objective must be assessed.

Even if militancy did reflect the class consciousness of striking workers, its use as an index of unionateness would require the assumption that all workers had the same cause and the same ability to strike. But this is obviously not so. Employers may be more considerate of some employees than of others. Some work groups enjoy a more strategic position in the process of production than others, and hence the strike may have greater efficacy for them. Paradoxically, such strategic work groups may not need to strike particularly often, if managements are sufficiently impressed by the threat alone. British printing workers are a case in point. Similarly, many professional associations are able to control their members' terms and conditions of employment without needing to resort to strike action or militant behaviour. As the Headmaster of Eton told the Headmasters' Conference in 1914, the absence of 'public utterances' by the Conference was not indicative of a lack of influence, as it might have been in the case of the National Union of Teachers. Rather, 'they were able to bring a great deal of influence to bear on those in authority in a very quiet way' (cited by *36*, p. 9). In contrast, most trade unions have to exercise their power in a highly visible way.

Blackburn himself recognizes the weakness of using militancy as an index of unionateness. In his words,

> The militancy of a union's behaviour depends on other factors besides its character. In the first place it depends on the opportunity and chances of success of such actions, which in turn are governed by the work and market situations as well as by the wealth and completeness of the union. Then it tends to be governed by the need for militancy, since the behaviour of the employer is always an important element in the situation. These factors are not part of character, and apart from completeness and to some extent wealth, they are largely out of an organisation's control in most cases (*15*, p. 31).

Consequently, he suggests that the militancy of an organization should be assessed not 'by the militancy of its actual actions', but by 'the extent to which it is prepared to use militant action ... the extent to which, when need arises, it displays readiness to take all forms of industrial action which may be effective' (p. 31). But how is willingness to be measured except by actions? And whose judgement is to be accepted as to which form of industrial action will prove most effective in a particular situation? As a measure of class consciousness the concept of militancy is not only conceptually and empirically dubious, it is also non-operational.

Affiliation to the Trades Union Congress and the Labour Party. Blackburn argues that affiliation to the T.U.C. is 'the most direct way of expressing shared interests and identity with other unions'. Affiliation 'entails an open acknowledgement of a trade-union character and voluntary participation in the trade-union movement' (p. 37). This may be the case, but it does not follow that affiliation to the T.U.C. is a measure of class consciousness. For a union's decision to affiliate is often motivated more by its organizational needs than by its degree of commitment to 'the general principles and ideology of trade unionism'.

This is made clear by the affiliation of certain major white-collar unions to the T.U.C. The National and Local Government Officers' Association and the three largest teachers' unions affiliated to the T.U.C. in the 1960s after creating and abandoning a separate white-collar congress, the Conference of Professional and Public Service Organisations. The decision in each case had little to do with any class consciousness which their members may have possessed. Rather, it was a response to the T.U.C.'s presence on the national planning bodies and C.O.P.P.S.O.'s exclusion from them. In consequence, these white-collar unions felt that by staying outside the T.U.C. they would have no access to policy-making bodies which directly affected their bargaining position (*36*, pp. 94–111). In the words of N.A.L.G.O.'s National Executive Council:

> So long as NALGO remains outside the T.U.C. it must become a powerless spectator on the sidelines. Only inside the T.U.C. has it any hope of influencing national economic and wages policy and adequately protecting its members (*237*, p. 69).

An additional danger of using affiliation to the T.U.C. as a criterion of unionateness is that it forces into the forefront of a union's character a decision normally taken years ago, and which for many unions involved merely the selection of an extra channel through which to pressure government. Thus as an index of class consciousness, this criterion at best distorts by over-emphasising the peripheral and at worst is totally irrelevant.

There are also serious objections to taking affiliation to the Labour Party as a measure of unionateness and hence class consciousness. Certainly the decision of the trade union movement to participate in the formation of the Labour Party had little to do with any commitment by unions to the creation of a socialist society. They were motivated not so much by a class conscious ideology as by their interest, especially after the Taff Vale Judgement in 1901, in legislation that would give them freedom and support in their industrial activities (*181*, pp. 260–4). In short, the union-socialist alliance started, as Allan Flanders has pointed out, 'as a marriage of convenience, with both parties adopting a very pragmatic attitude to the advantages which each of them could gain from living together. And so, in its essentials, it has always remained' (*67*, p. 33).

Indeed, there have been periods in which some of the most militant and politically conscious trade unionists have eschewed parliamentary political action altogether. In Britain, as in France, the syndicalists stressed the self-sufficiency of the trade union movement. They believed, as Ridley has pointed out about the French syndicalists, that political parties and political action 'misled the workers, wasted their energy in the *cul-de-sac* of parliamentary intrigue and distracted them from the real struggle' (*190*, p. 91). In place of the party, they put the trade union, 'the autonomous organisation of the working class' which is 'wholly proletarian in character and excludes mere sympathisers' (p. 173). And in place of political action, they put the doctrine of direct industrial action, the belief that the emancipation of the proletariat 'must be achieved by the workers acting as workers and without intermediaries'. In short, the syndicalists believed that 'just as the union is the proper form of organisation for the proletariat, so the industrial sphere is its proper field of action' (p. 174).

Since there are many prescriptions for union political

action besides the social-democratic one proposed by Blackburn and Lockwood, it is perhaps not surprising that the relationship which exists in Britain between the trade union movement and the Labour Party has no easy parallel in many other countries. As Pickles has pointed out,

> In France there are four trade union confederations (in addition to one for supervisory staffs and a politically independent one, largely for teachers), representing respectively pure anarcho-syndicalism, Christian (largely Catholic) social and political action, communism, and diluted syndicalism. Diverse, though less numerous, political attitudes are also found in Italy, Belgium and some other countries. Nobody in these countries even dreams any longer of a united trade union movement, much less of a political party based on such a movement. The notion that trade unionism is in some way inherently linked with socialism—a notion that is probably more deeply rooted because it is so often inarticulate—is no less insular. The only country outside the British tradition in which there exists an organic link between the trade union movement and the socialist party is Norway. In Belgium, the organic link which existed before the Second World War has since been severed. In Germany, though the D.G.B. (central trade union organisation) lends general support to the S.P.D. (Social Democratic Party) it is careful to avoid any formal connection, and roughly similar situations are to be found in some of the smaller European countries (*181*, pp. 258–9).

Yet the history of European unionism hardly suggests a lower level of 'unionateness' in terms of the other six criteria than British unionism.

Thus to state that unionateness increases with affiliation to the Labour Party is to close off the whole question of the relationship between political and industrial activity, to assume the primacy of the social democratic prescription for union politics, to rely almost entirely upon the British political tradition, to grant to the

Labour Party an overriding dedication to the interests of organized labour that is hard to maintain before the Labour Government of 1964 and even more difficult to argue after that date, and to fail to bring out that unions face a choice of mode of political activity, a choice constantly to be re-examined in the light of changing circumstances.

Members versus leaders. The above review of the seven criteria of unionateness suggests that they do not provide an accurate or unambiguous measure of class consciousness. But even granted for the moment that they do, it is still debatable whose class consciousness they measure. To assume that they measure the class consciousness of members is to ignore the political process within unions and to overstate the degree to which the attitudes of the leadership can be used as a guide to those of the membership. Although membership attitudes are no doubt a constraint on leadership behaviour, there is abundant evidence to indicate the lack of congruence between the two. Lockwood documented this for the National Union of Clerks: 'The low degree of political interest displayed by the mass of the membership contrasts strangely with the outlook of the leadership of the NUC which was extremely active in this sphere during the thirties' (*150*, p. 167). Nor is this merely a phenomenon of the inter-war period; it reappeared in the context of unilateralism in 1959. A national survey found only 16 per cent of trade unionists in favour of a unilateral surrender of nuclear weapons, but at the Labour Party Conference this was backed by a majority of the delegates representing the trade unions (*212*, p. 12). Other examples could be given, but this is probably not necessary. For sociologists are increasingly becoming aware that membership goals differ from leadership goals, and it is the latter which tend to be taken as organizational goals. Hence any class consciousness reflected by a union's character is more likely to be attributable to its leadership than to its general membership.

Measurement and weighting. But even if it could be granted that the seven criteria discussed above actually did measure the class consciousness of union members, the concept of unionateness would still present some formidable operational problems. The seven criteria can be divided into two groups: the first group includes items one to three which are continuous variables, while the second group includes items four to seven which are discrete variables. The first problem is to establish appropriate scales of measurement for the different types of variables. There is then the problem of the relative weighting of the seven items, especially since they are of different types, to provide an overall index of unionateness. For example, since there need not be any concurrence of industrial and political militancy, how industrially militant must a union be to offset its lack of affiliation to the Labour Party? Finally, since it is unionization, or unionateness and completeness jointly, which is supposed to reflect class consciousness, there is the problem of the relative weighting to be assigned to these two items. Blackburn is aware of all these problems and admits that it would require a considerable development of the theory of unionateness to overcome them (*15*, pp. 19, 46–7, 239, n. 1). But it is difficult to see how the weighting problems, and perhaps even the measurement problems, could be overcome except by the researcher exercising his purely subjective judgement.

Specification of class consciousness. A fundamental problem underlying the assessment of the above argument is that its advocates have not made clear exactly what they mean by class consciousness. It is surprising and unfortunate that nowhere in a body of literature asserting a central relationship between union character and class consciousness is the nature of the latter adequately specified.

In discussing the relationship between union character and class consciousness, both Lockwood (*150*, pp. 195–7) and Blackburn (*15*, pp. 19–20) distinguish between different types of interests: 'immediate', 'instrumental', and 'ideological'. Lockwood defines immediate interests as those 'particular economic aims of a union with regard to such matters as salaries, hours, holidays, promotion and superannuation'. He sees these giving rise to instrumental interests 'which are common to all unions of employees: matters such as the legal status of trade unionism, victimization, recognition, strike action, negotiation machinery, political representation and the like'. Blackburn does not refer to immediate interests, but broadly agrees with Lockwood's conception of instrumental interests being concerned with 'effectiveness'. Ideological interests, according to Lockwood, are 'of a political kind, all the principles and assumptions arising out of the connection between the trade union movement and the Labour Party'. Blackburn feels that this use of 'ideological' is 'somewhat restricted', and he suggests that attitudes to aspects of union character other than affiliation to the Labour Party 'may properly be described as ideological without necessarily having political implications'.

This categorization of interests is unhelpful for at least three reasons. To begin with, it draws a false distinction between instrumentalities and ideologies. Instrumental interests should be contrasted, as C. Wright Mills has done, with non-instrumental or principled interests (*170*, pp. 307–8). Organizations and individuals pursue the former as a means to an end, as a way of promoting their own self-interest; they pursue the latter as ends in themselves and with no concern for their effect on self-interest. The pursuit of either type of interests presupposes the possession of some set of beliefs about society and may therefore be regarded as deriving from an ideology.

Secondly, even as restated by Mills, this categorization of interests is unhelpful because it is non-operational. Although the distinction between instrumental and principled interests may be analytically useful, it is virtually impossible to distinguish between the two in practice. For, as Blackburn admits, both instrumental and principled considerations may be relevant in determining any of the items of unionateness, and there is no way of unambiguously isolating the precise form of motivation from the behaviour of unions.

Finally, even if the operational difficulty could be overcome, this categorization would still be unhelpful within the context of a discussion of class consciousness. For the problem is not whether particular aspects of union behaviour are motivated by principled or instrumental considerations, but rather whether the ideology within which those motives are defined is itself class conscious in nature. The solution to this problem requires that the nature of class consciousness be exactly and explicitly specified.

Blackburn fails to do this. In spite of the title of his book,* he says relatively little about class and class consciousness. The closest he comes to defining class consciousness is in discussing the character of staff associations in banking. He points out that they have

> no sense of class solidarity, no sense of a common interest or need to co-operate with other workers, except to a limited extent with employees of other banks, and certainly no sense of a need to participate in the political side of the labour movement. Instead they have an internalist, almost 'isolationist', middle-class ideology (*15*, p. 110).

This would seem to imply that for Blackburn the defi-

---

* The book is entitled *Union Character and Social Class*. But it is more accurately described by the title of the Ph.d thesis upon which it is based: *Unionisation and Union Character in Banking*, University of Liverpool, 1966.

nitive characteristic of class consciousness is a recognition by employees of their common interests and need to co-operate with each other. Inasmuch as this is Blackburn's view, it would seem to derive from Lockwood's much more explicit and detailed specification of class consciousness.

Lockwood argues that

> The conditions making for concerted action among the members of an occupational group and those making for class consciousness are not identical. Concerted action is a function of the recognition by the members of the occupational group that they have interests in common; class consciousness entails the further realization that certain of those interests are also shared by other groups of employees (*150*, p. 137).

He further elaborates this statement with respect to clerical workers by suggesting that

> class consciousness may be said to emerge when the members of a clerical association realize, first, that their common interests are engendered by the conflict of interest between employer and employee, and secondly, that their common interests are not fundamentally dissimilar in type from those underlying the concerted actions of manual workers (p. 137).

Although Lockwood makes the most serious attempt of all the writers surveyed to specify the nature of class consciousness, he nowhere fully or explicitly lays out the actual set of beliefs that for him constitute class consciousness. Consequently, his specification raises more questions than it answers. What exactly are the 'certain' interests which an occupational group must realize are shared by other groups of employees before it can be said to be conscious of class ties? How 'fundamentally dissimilar' can interests be seen to be before class consciousness can be said not to exist? Why must clerical workers identify with manual workers in order to be class conscious? And if class consciousness amongst cleri-cal workers requires feelings of solidarity and shared interests with manual workers, can manual workers be said to be class conscious, as Lockwood implies, even though they have generally been as hostile to white-collar workers as white-collar workers have been to them?

With which employees an occupational group must see its interests being shared before it can be said to be class conscious, obviously depends upon how the con-cept of class is defined. If class is defined in a Marxist fashion and the proletariat is taken to include all em-ployees who are divorced from the ownership and control of the means of production and are obliged to sell their labour-power in order to make a livelihood, then white-collar employees are obviously members of the prole-tariat and must identify with other proletarians, including manual workers, in order to be class conscious. But Lockwood argues, as does Blackburn, for defining class position to include the following factors:

> First, 'market situation', that is to say the economic posi-tion narrowly conceived, consisting of source and size of income, degree of job-security, and opportunity for up-ward occupational mobility. Secondly, 'work situation', the set of social relationships in which the individual is involved at work by virtue of his position in the division of labour. And finally, 'status situation', or the position of the individual in the hierarchy of prestige in the society at large. The experiences originating in these three spheres may be seen as the principal determinants of class consciousness (p. 15).

Indeed, he concludes that 'as soon as the term "class situation" is understood to cover not only market situa-tion but also work situation, it is clear that clerk and manual worker do not, in most cases, share the same class situation at all' (p. 208). Given this, the clerk who identi-fies with manual workers is less class conscious than the clerk who identifies with other white-collar or 'middle class' employees. Paradoxically, Lockwood can only claim that this is not so if he is prepared to accept the Marxian definition of class which he has so forcefully rejected.

To claim that the trade union movement is 'the main vehicle of working-class consciousness' and that 'to the extent that clerical workers become involved in trade unionism they have to come to terms with its wider class character' (pp. 13, 137), defined in the way that Lockwood and Blackburn do, is to begin to hint at the set of beliefs and orientations which for them constitute class consciousness. By singling out collective bargaining and industrial and political co-operation with manual unions through the Trades Union Congress and the Labour Party as the appropriate ways of advancing the interests of white-collar employees, they would appear to be suggesting that class consciousness should be defined within a social democratic frame of reference.

This may well be so. But by treating class consciousness in this way, Lockwood and Blackburn fail to recognize that there are many diverse views regarding the nature of trade unionism, of class consciousness, and of the relationship between them. By suggesting that class consciousness no longer requires any revolutionary content, Lockwood and Blackburn adopt a particular position in a long standing debate between Marxist and non-Marxist scholars on the nature of capitalism and on the character and historical potential of the working class and its organizations.* By suggesting that there are 'general principles and ideology of trade unionism', they fail to recognize that

> Seen from the standpoint of aims, ideals, methods, and theories, there is no normal type to which all union vari-

* For an excellent critical discussion of the views on trade unionism of Gramsci, Lenin, and other Marxist writers see Hyman (*117*).

ants approximate, no single labor movement which has progressively adapted itself to progressive change of circumstances, no one set of postulates which can be spoken of as *the* philosophy of unionism (*54*, p. xxiii).

In short, by failing to consider the diversity of views on the question of trade unionism and class consciousness, Lockwood and Blackburn in effect close off by academic fiat a central area of debate in modern sociological analysis.

Yet regardless of whether class consciousness is defined in a reformist or revolutionary fashion, it cannot be unambiguously measured by unionateness. For, as this chapter has demonstrated, the decision of a union to adopt any one of the seven dimensions of unionateness need not reflect an assessment of wider class interests and solidarity or even a narrower trade union consciousness in Blackburn's sense of a commitment 'to the general principles and ideology of trade unionism'. All the decision needs to and often does reflect is an assessment of the narrowly conceived organizational requirements of the union and the sectional needs of its members. Hence nothing about class consciousness can be deduced from the decision itself but only from a detailed examination of the factors which motivate the decision in each case. In the absence of such an examination, unionateness is nothing more than a formula with little explanatory power and operational value.

Unionization, character, and completeness. This conclusion leads back to the question of union growth. Blackburn points out that unionization is usually measured by its size in terms of completeness or density, but claims that this is 'inadequate as, without reference to character, it tells us nothing of the significance of the size' (*15*, p. 43). Hence, in his view, 'unionisation, the measure of social significance, cannot be understood independently of union character' (p. 10). If unionization is seen as being socially significant primarily because it is taken to be an index of class consciousness, and if this consciousness is held to be mainly determined or at least reflected by union character rather than size, then it obviously follows that the latter should not be considered separately from the former. But, if as this chapter has demonstrated, union character and the unionization of which it is an element cannot be assumed to measure class consciousness, then it follows that union character and size need not be considered together.

But Blackburn offers another reason why it is not possible to attach any significance or give any meaning whatsoever to size without referring to character: 'character must be included in order that we may know what completeness is measuring' (pp. 13, 232). Obviously, without a clear and consistent definition of a union, it is not possible to identify accurately the organizations whose completeness is to be assessed. And since any satisfactory definition must by its very nature refer to some fundamental characteristic of a union, it follows that the size of unionization cannot be measured without some reference to character.

It does not follow, however, that union character needs to be defined in the manner specified by Blackburn before the organizations whose size is to be measured can be identified. For it does not follow that all or even any of the aspects of character which he specifies are essential to defining a trade union. In fact, Blackburn himself seems to suggest that collective bargaining is the only one of his seven items of unionateness which is actually basic to the concept of a union. He claims that collective bargaining is the 'definitive' function of a union and 'if an organisation has no score under this item it has no score under the other items, i.e. its level of unionateness is zero' (pp. 21, 28). But, as this chapter has already pointed out, collective bargaining is not so much a definitive as a derivative function. For it derives from the more basic function of participating in job regulation, and it is only one of three ways in which unions can do this. In addition to participating in job regulation jointly with employers, a method usually referred to as collective bargaining, unions may do it trilaterally with employers and public representatives or unilaterally by 'binding their members to observe working rules which the "other side" has had no say in making'.* Thus participation in job regulation is the definitive characteristic of a trade union, and hence a union may be defined as any organization of employees which participates or attempts to participate by any means in the process of making and administering the rules by which its members are regulated on the job.

Blackburn's mistake in defining unionateness is to confuse what Flanders has called 'the body and the spirit of trade unions' (*163*). All unions share a common basic objective: to participate in some form of job regulation. In addition to this common function which may be likened to the common bodily functions of men, each union has individual characteristics which may be termed its 'spirit'. And just as it is possible and useful to define a man and measure his size without referring to the various individual personality traits which go to make up his spirit, so it is possible and useful to define a union and measure its size without referring to all the various individual aspects of its character.

Blackburn argues against defining a union in terms of its common basic function of job regulation, or, to use his words, of 'protecting and furthering the interests of its members, as employees'. He admits that to define a union in this way would be 'convenient', but he claims that 'it would extend the meaning of the term far beyond what is usual' (*15*, p. 14). This argument is unpersuasive. Blackburn's own definition, by covering professional associations such as the British Medical Association

* See Flanders (*66*, pp. 21–8) for a discussion of the concepts of job regulation and collective bargaining.

which engage in collective bargaining, already extends the meaning of 'union' beyond what many people would regard as 'usual'. Indeed, the plea for a wider definition of unionism which lies at the basis of Blackburn's argument is its greatest strength. Its weakness is that it does not go far enough and thereby forces the social investigator to make subjective judgements about the appropriateness of various methods of job regulation.

The third and final reason offered by Blackburn for claiming that the size of a union cannot be understood independently of its character is indicated by his formula—unionization = unionateness × completeness—which suggests that unionateness and completeness are inversely related for a given level of unionization. Since the three variables which enter this formula are defined to be related in this way, it is merely a tautology. That is, given the limiting mathematical conditions which Blackburn posits (p. 44), then for any given degree of unionization, completeness and unionateness *must* vary inversely. But Blackburn regards this formula as a 'hypothesis' rather than as a tautology. It can only be a hypothesis, however, if the relationship it specifies does not hold by definition. That is, the formula must be capable of being proved or disproved. As Blackburn himself points out, 'there must be established a corresponding empirical relationship before the formula can be regarded as sociologically valid' (p. 43).

Blackburn fails to establish such a relationship. The measurement and weighting problems associated with the concepts of unionateness and unionization (*supra*, p. 96) make them hard to quantify, and hence it is difficult to establish a precise or rigorous empirical relationship between them. Even allowing for this difficulty, however, Blackburn does not prove his case. On the contrary, his banking evidence suggests that 'character is not a main determinant of decisions to join' either the union or the staff associations (p. 264). Moreover, inasmuch as he does identify the determinants of character and completeness, he points to variables such as employer attitudes and policies which lie outside his formula. In short, Blackburn fails to establish empirically that character and completeness are inversely related or that they are even significantly related at all.*

This conclusion is not meant to imply that character and completeness are never related. For even the most cursory reading of labour history reveals that they sometimes are. All that is being suggested here is that they are not always related: the relationship is problematic rather than axiomatic. Moreover, there is no empirical justification for giving primacy of place to character as a determinant of completeness or to completeness as a determinant of character. There are other potential determinants such as employer attitudes and policies which may have a more important impact on character and completeness than either of them do on each other. Hence there is no more reason to treat character and completeness as being inseparably linked than there is to treat either or both of them as being inseparably linked to any of these other potential determinants.

Finally, this critique of Blackburn's argument is not meant to imply that size alone is sufficient to give an understanding of trade unions, or that this is the only aspect of unions which is worth considering. Union character is also important. Indeed, it is even more important than Blackburn suggests. He claims that 'once we have described the character it is of little further interest or importance unless it has some bearing on whether or not people join an organisation' (p. 43). But it is difficult to see why this should be so. Regardless of

---

* Blackburn does show that the character of the employee organizations in banking have been important in relation to the attitudes of employers. But since the character of the staff associations have been largely shaped by the employers, it is not clear to what extent their character has an impact on completeness independently of the influence of employer attitudes and policies.

what relationship may exist between union growth and character, it is valid, interesting, and necessary to assess the characters of different unions, to explain why they differ, and to ascertain what impact character has on various aspects of union behaviour. Union character is a question in its own right, and there is no reason to link it uniquely with the question of union growth.

IV. CONCLUSION

This chapter has demonstrated that differences between the characters of manual unions, white-collar unions, and professional associations are more those of degree than of kind and are not significantly related to differences in their members' social positions. It has also shown that the character of a union, at least as defined by Lockwood and Blackburn, is an inaccurate, ambiguous, and inoperable index of any feeling of class or trade union consciousness which its members may possess.

Given these findings, it is tempting to conclude that there is no relationship whatsoever between social stratification and union character. But there are at least three reasons why such a conclusion would be unjustified. To begin with, virtually any aspect of a union's goals, structure, or behaviour may be taken as a dimension of its character, and if dimensions other than those specified by Lockwood and Blackburn were considered, they might conceivably be found to be significantly related to some feature of the social stratification system.

Secondly, a union's character may be analysed not only at the national level, as the literature surveyed above has tended to do, but also at the level of the work group, the branch, the district, the region, and the trade group, and it may vary from one level to another. Hence the absence of a significant relationship between social stratification and union character at the national level does not prevent such a relationship existing at other levels. In fact, the national level of union character is the least likely to be related to the social positions or perspectives of union members. For the political process within a union tends to ensure that this is the level of union activity over which members have the least influence and control. If there is any relationship between social stratification and union character at the national level, it is likely to be the social positions and perspectives of union leaders rather than those of union members which are important. But this is a possibility which the literature surveyed above does not examine. Nor does it examine the possibility that the social positions and perspectives of union members may be an important determinant of union character at less aggregative levels where the political process is less likely to intervene significantly between the character of the union and that of its membership.

Finally, any relationship which exists between social stratification and union character must by its very nature be highly contingent. For a union's goals and behaviour, the social positions and perceptions of its members, and the relationship between these variables are unlikely to remain constant under all circumstances. On the contrary, they are likely to vary from one historical, social, and cultural context to another. Hence to conclude that there is never a significant relationship between social stratification and union character would have as little justification as to suggest, as has most of the literature surveyed above, that there is always such a relationship. Whatever the nature of the relationship which exists between social stratification and union character at any moment of time, it is not simple, firm, and static but complex, tenuous, and fluid.

4

Social Imagery

The general conclusion which emerges from the two previous chapters is that the various social stratification models advanced by theorists to explain trade unionism fail to do so. The available evidence suggests that there is no simple or constant relationship between social position and either union growth or union character, and that neither of these, taken singly or jointly, provide an adequate indicator of the class consciousness of union members. But the evidence only demonstrates that the models do not correspond to reality; it does not fully explain why. This requires an analysis of the premises upon which the models are based. In particular, the link they postulate, on the one hand, between social position and social imagery and, on the other hand, between social imagery and trade unionism must be examined in greater detail.

The literature on social imagery is now extensive and it is worth emphasizing the statement made in Chapter 1 that this study is not concerned to give it a full exposition or to subject it to a full critique. Rather, this chapter will focus on the treatment of social imagery by writers concerned to establish a connection between trade unionism and social stratification. In discussing the adequacy of their treatment, the argument necessarily moves into this wider discussion of social imagery. But its contribution to this debate is at best marginal. For while the wider debate on social imagery has moved far beyond the simple polarities that abound in the debate on trade unionism and social stratification, it is with these simple polarities that this chapter must be primarily concerned. Moreover, what this chapter has to say will be very tentative, not least because so much of the literaure with which it has to deal is methodologically weak and draws too heavily on attitude surveys taken from too narrow a period of time, the late 1950s and early 1960s.

I. SOCIAL POSITION AND SOCIAL IMAGERY

Most of the stratification models examined in the previous chapters are based upon the assumption that there are two predominant types of social imagery—a status ideology and a class ideology—the former generally being held more or less exclusively by white-collar and professional workers or those higher in the stratification system, and the latter by manual workers or those lower down the social hierarchy. But the available evidence does not support this assumption. Rather, it suggests that there are many manual workers who hold elements of a status ideology, just as there are many white-collar and professional workers who hold elements of a class ideology.

The Status Ideology And Manual Workers

The writers who have used the notion of a status ideology in the explanation of trade unionism have understood those who hold it to support, or at least acquiesce in, the existing distribution of power and rewards in society, and to see the relationships between various social groups as being essentially harmonistic. At the industrial as opposed to the societal level those holding a status ideology tend to identify with 'management' and to have a harmonistic conception of employer-employee relationships. In addition, individualism is seen as being intrinsically valuable, and individual ascent up the occupational or organizational hierarchy according to individual merit is stressed. In short, as Chapter 1 made clear, the status ideology is portrayed as being composed of two major value complexes—harmony and individualism.

Harmony. There is considerable evidence which demonstrates that a harmonistic conception of social relationships is not exclusive to white-collar workers but is also held by many manual workers. The areas in which this can be shown include the degree of acceptance of the existing distribution of income, and the degree of legitimacy assigned to the existing distribution of power not only within society at large but also within industry.

The extent to which some manual workers have at certain times accepted the existing distribution of income can be illustrated by quoting the results of some recent social surveys. Samuel found that most of his sample of manual workers from Stevenage and Clapham tended to be satisfied with their relative economic position. They were particularly prone to make favourable comparisons with their own less prosperous past, rather than to make unfavourable comparisons between their own present position and those of other groups higher in the social structure (*198*, p. 10). Similarly, Runciman found that the comparative reference groups of most of the manual workers in his national sample tended to be very much restricted to groups adjacent to themselves in the social hierarchy. Their frame of reference for comparative purposes rarely crossed the manual/non-manual boundary to include white-collar workers. In fact, he found that 27 per cent of the manual workers could not think of any category doing better economically than themselves. He concluded that 'both the magnitude and frequency of relative deprivation among manual workers and their wives are very much lower than would accord with the facts of economic inequality' (*196*, pp. 192, 217).

There would also seem to be many manual workers

who are not particularly disturbed over the existing distribution of power in society. This discovery is not
exactly new. In 1889 Engels remarked that the 'most
repulsive thing' in Britain 'is the bourgeois "respectabil-
ity" which has grown deep into the bones of the workers'
(cited by *151*, p. 248). Indeed, the existence of a group
of 'working-class Tories' who hold 'deferential' attitudes
towards the established political elite has for a long time
been regarded as one explanation of the continued
dominance of the Conservative Party despite the numeri-
cal strength of manual workers in the population.

Recent evidence suggests that the acceptance of the
existing power structure by manual workers is even more
widespread than was previously imagined. Several
studies have revealed that a substantial proportion of
manual workers believe that those at the top of the social
hierarchy are better equipped to rule, either by birth or
education, than those lower in the hierarchy. Moreover,
many who hold this view identify themselves as 'working-
class' and vote for the Labour Party. As Nordlinger has
remarked on the basis of a national sample carried out
in 1963 among male manual workers:

> The unmistakable conclusion which emerges from the
> discussion ... is that the marked upper class and aristo-
> cratic strains in the English political culture are strongly
> infused in the working-class political culture.... Not only
> do a significant proportion of these ... groups prefer to
> have men with high status as political leaders. Even
> among those workers who subscribe to an achievement or
> class orientation, and who consequently are prone to be
> critical of various aspects of the social stratification system,
> there is a hearty respect and admiration for high born,
> well bred and exclusively educated men as political
> leaders (*174*, p. 81).

McKenzie and Silver found that one-third of their
sample of urban manual workers had no image of class
conflict at all. Even those who did perceive conflict in

social relationships, generally saw it as a temporary intrusion into a basically harmonious situation and not as
an endemic feature of society. That is, many 'working
class voters are more likely to see conflict as artificially
stimulated and unnecessary than as an inevitable consequence of conflicting social goals' (*165*, p. 137). Similarly, Goldthorpe and his colleagues found that among
their sample of 'affluent' manual workers from the motor
industry of Luton the idea of society as

> fundamentally divided into opposing classes was only very
> rarely advanced. The class structure was not, as they des-
> cribed it, a historically created system of domination
> which had to be overthrown, or at any rate combated, in
> order for men such as themselves to achieve their legiti-
> mate objectives. More usually, one could say, it was rep-
> resented as a basic *datum* of social existence—as a natural
> rather than as a man-made phenomenon, which indi-
> viduals had in the main to accept and adapt to (*88*, p.
> 154).

Even in the industrial context where the class ideology
might be thought to be more manifest and the 'sides'
more clearly apparent, there is evidence to show that
such an ideology is not universally held among manual
workers and it is not necessarily generalized to all aspects of the relationship with management. Goldthorpe
and his colleagues found that although most of the
manual workers in their sample were aware of conflicts
of interest over the relationship between 'effort' and
'reward' and over the distribution of the fruits of co-
operation, a functionally interdependent view of relationships between management and workers was
predominant. In their words,

> The image of the enterprise which is represented here
> is one which contrasts sharply with the far more 'dichoto-
> mous' views, stressing antagonism and exploitation, which
> have been well documented in the case of miners, dockers
> and other industrial workers characterised by a more

solidaristic orientation and by a relatively highly developed class consciousness. In fact, our affluent workers seem little more likely than the men in the white-collar sample to interpret management-worker relations primarily in 'oppositional' terms (*86*, p. 74).*

Similarly, Cotgrove and Vamplew found among a sample of affluent process workers that a harmonious view of the enterprise coexisted with conflict over the wage-effort bargain (*40*, pp. 182–3).

Nor is this view of employer-employee relationships necessarily confined to 'affluent' manual workers. A study of manual workers in shipbuilding and other industries in Wallsend, a 'traditional working-class' community, revealed that even among the 'traditional proletariat' the class ideology is by no means homogeneous or universal (*24*). When asked an open question on what they thought of 'top management', only 48 per cent of the replies were generally unfavourable, 31 per cent were favourable, and the rest were non-committal. And contrary to assumptions generally held about the traditional working class, 75 per cent of the shipbuilders had a generally favourable attitude when specifically referring to their immediate supervisors. Moreover, a considerable majority of the apprentices in the sample held a co-operative view of the enterprise, and over 50 per cent of them said they would welcome the idea of moving into management although they thought the prospects of doing so were slight.

Even among such 'traditional' manual workers as dockers, a conflict view of employer-employee relationships does not necessarily predominate. Hill found

---

* This is not to deny, as Westergaard has observed, that 'in fact there is a fair amount of evidence . . . to show that "social criticism" co-exists with "social apathy" in contemporary British working class consciousness. The essence of this consciousness is precisely its ambivalence and internal contradictions' (*243*, p. 121). The purpose of the argument here is merely to stress that the evidence will not allow a simple equation of manual workers and a class ideology.

among a sample of London dockers that 75 per cent of them thought 'there were reasonable personal relationships, without conflict, between the men and managers in their respective firms'. When asked to choose between the idea 'of a firm as a football team (where teamwork means success and is to the advantage of all), as opposed to the idea that teamwork is impossible because management and men are on opposite sides', 56 per cent chose the 'harmonious' image. And of the minority who gave a 'conflict' response, only 10 per cent thought that 'this was inherent in the nature of employment relationships as such' (*105*, p. 339).

Individualism. There is also evidence which indicates that individualistic aspirations are not uncommon among manual workers. The 'Horatio Alger' myth of unlimited individual opportunity which Strauss (*217*) claims is typical of American white-collar workers, also seems to retain its magic for some manual workers. Chinoy (*33*, pp. 86–93) found that many American manual workers aspire to individual mobility not through promotion within a bureaucratic hierarchy, but through such traditional 'heroic frontier' methods as owning their own business. For some, these are only dreams with little possibility of fulfilment. But a considerable number of American manual workers still take this route to individual 'success' as indicated by the high turnover in small business ownership among manual workers in the United States. Similarly, Goldthorpe and his colleagues found that the dream of escape from the 'tyranny' of the mass production process by small business ownership was expressed by 73 per cent of the manual workers in their sample although only a minority regarded it as a serious proposition (*86*, p. 132). Whether a dream or a realistic possibility, it is the desire to escape the consequences of mass production via an individual rather than a collective solution that is significant in this context.

Moreover, the unit of advancement for some manual workers is not the 'working class' as a whole as the class ideology model suggests, but rather the advancement of the nuclear family as a unit. Goldthorpe and his colleagues found that most of the manual workers in their sample had an 'awareness of themselves as carrying through some individual, or more probably family, project', and an 'awareness of being engaged in a course of action aimed at effecting some basic change in their life situation and, perhaps, in their social identity' (p. 177). Similarly, Runciman found that many of the manual workers in his sample had frustrated individualistic ambitions which they projected on to their children and which took the form of individual or family 'projects'. For example, 82 per cent of his manual respondents, only 6 per cent less than his white-collar respondents, wanted a university education for their children (*196*, p. 230).

Whether or not manual workers are as likely to have individual as collective aspirations in society at large, it has been strongly argued that in the context of the work situation they are much more likely to reject individualism for collectivism. Several studies (*1*; *11*) have demonstrated that opportunities for individual promotion for manual workers within the bureaucratic hierarchy are quite restricted, and that relatively few of them actually apply for promotion or even think of applying. But this rejection of individual promotion is not necessarily a principled decision as has often been implied by those who attribute a class ideology to manual workers. Many manual workers refuse to apply to be foremen not because they feel they would be moving to the 'other side', but because of the highly instrumental consideration that the extra responsibility involved in being a foreman is not adequately compensated for in terms of pay. Promotion, as Goldthorpe and his colleagues found among their sample of 'affluent' workers, is not 'widely rejected out of group or class solidarity', but is 'critically assessed in terms of its costs and rewards in relation to the individual's present work situation' (*86*, p. 130).

Nor is promotion the only mode of individual advancement open to manual workers. In many industries such as steel and motor manufacture there are formally or informally established job hierarchies in which individuals either compete or become eligible according to certain generally accepted criteria for the better jobs. And although the prospects for vertical mobility may be low, this does not apply to horizontal mobility between firms, particularly in the case of craftsmen whose skills are often readily transferable.

There are also other ways in which manual workers express individualistic aspirations within the work situation. Sykes, having elsewhere stressed the strong sense of individualism among white-collar workers, found among a sample of 'navvies' in the civil engineering industry that great importance was attached to individual independence and lack of permanent attachment to either employers, unions, or even fellow employees. The solution to any kind of grievance was to seek work elsewhere rather than to attempt to remedy the situation collectively in the offending work situation. The navvies stated that

> every man ought to be able to look after himself and his interests without help from anyone .... Belonging to a trade union temporarily on the particular job they thought harmless. Belonging to a trade union *permanently* was much the same as belonging to an employer: both are states of dependence which no real man could accept .... In short, the navvies regarded trade unions not as *their own* organisations but as external bodies membership of which was incompatible with their independence as individuals (*226*, pp. 27–8).

Similar individualistic orientations, although not so extreme in their form, were observed by Lupton among manual workers in a garment factory. The general attitude was that 'you have to look after No. 1'. There was little collective control over the work situation even though the employees were unionized. The major strategy for dealing with grievances was to threaten to leave or to go absent, and, if conditions became intolerable, to leave altogether (*154*, p. 92).

The Class Ideology and White-Collar and Professional Workers

The writers who have used the notion of a class ideology in the explanation of trade unionism have understood those who hold it to reject the existing distribution of power, facilities, and rewards; to see society as being composed of two conflicting interests—those who have power and those who do not; and to see employer-employee relationships as being antagonistic. They are also assumed to perceive the major means of personal advancement as the collective ascent of their class as a whole by means of collective action. The stratification models being considered in this study generally assume that this ideology is held more or less exclusively by manual workers. The above evidence has already demonstrated that certain of its elements are not held by some manual workers. There is also evidence to show that the major value complexes of the alternative status ideology—harmony and individualism—are not adhered to by many white-collar workers. Rather, their orientations reveal elements of conflict and collectivism.

Conflict. Evidence generated by recent social surveys suggests that white-collar workers are not all that happy with the current distribution of rewards in society. Runciman found that they were much more dissatisfied with their relative economic position than were manual workers, and that the former were also much more concerned about the relative prosperity of other groups than were the latter. As Runciman says, 'the non-manual respondents were not only more likely to see some other group as doing better, but more likely, if they did so, to disapprove' (*196*, p. 197). Indeed, the white-collar workers in the sample were more likely to experience 'fraternalistic' deprivation on behalf of their 'class' as a whole than manual workers who, if they made comparisons with others at all, tended to compare themselves to individuals within their own 'class' rather than to make comparisons between different classes. A study by Mercer and Weir of white-collar workers revealed that in addition to being concerned about their salaries, a majority of them felt that their companies could afford to pay them more and that this should come from excess profits and increased efficiency (*166*, p. 122).

Mercer and Weir also found, as the social stratification models predict, that between 51 and 62 per cent of their various white-collar groups perceived the relationship between management and workers as being akin to membership of a common 'team' and only 20 to 30 per cent saw these relationships in terms of conflicting 'sides'. But on closer examination the 'team' images divided into two groups: a large majority were simply referring to the functional interdependence between the various groups or roles within the company, and only 11 to 22 per cent of the whole sample were referring to a more affectively based moral involvement—a 'co-operative' or harmonious spirit (pp. 120–1).

Mercer and Weir's study also reveals that white-collar employees do not necessarily accept the legitimacy of all aspects of management. Between 23 and 33 per cent of those interviewed in the private companies in the sample believed that management personnel had gained their positions by 'illegitimate' means (p. 122); in other words, these white-collar workers believed that appropriate criteria such as education or competence had not

been utilized or fully adhered to. Moreover, a considerable desire for autonomy and for some control over decision making was also expressed by the white-collar
workers in the sample. 'Effective consultation with
management at all levels' was rated by between 52 and
71 per cent of them as one of the most important
functions which a trade union could fulfil, second only
to negotiating over salaries (p. 131). This would indicate,
contrary to the suppositions of the status ideology, that
these white-collar workers were unwilling to accept
management's decisions as being necessarily in their own
interests, or, indeed, to accept that such decisions lay
entirely within the prerogative of managerial personnel.

Even professionals are not as addicted to the status
ideology as is commonly imagined. To begin with, the
'professional ethic' which is supposed to reinforce the
status ideology among professional workers does not
appear to have much meaning for many of them. Certain
groups commonly regarded as professional do not seem
to possess a sense of corporate identity, a set of values
which corresponds to the stereotype of the 'professional
ethic', or even a consensus as to the meaning of the term
'professional'.

Seidman and Cain (202, pp. 252–3) found among a
sample of qualified engineers that while 'professionalism'
was identified by some with individual advancement
according to merit and by others with fee-paid practitioners and hence of little relevance to themselves, the
majority had little conception of its meaning beyond the
possession of certain formal qualifications. Similarly,
Goldstein found that most of his sample of engineers
simply saw their 'professionalism' as meaning that they
had a qualification or licence to practise. He notes that
'there appeared to be little conceptualization beyond
this point—certainly nothing the professional societies
themselves would have recognized as part of their outlook'. While there was 'some groping beyond the simple

technical requirement for professional status' among a few individuals, 'there was little reference to a code of ethics, and little concern with the professional societies' (*78*, pp. 98, 106). The findings of these American studies are supported in Britain by Ellis' survey of industrial and academic scientists and technologists. Only 58 per cent of the sample saw themselves as 'professional' in any sense whatsoever, and between 67 and 73 per cent of these saw it simply in terms of the possession of a qualification (*62*, pp. 185, 189).

Even among employees for whom the 'professional ethic' does have meaning, however, it need not necessarily reinforce the harmonistic image of employer-employee relationships characteristic of the status ideology. It may do just the opposite. Over fifty years ago Thorstein Veblen (*236*) argued that a fundamental conflict existed between the pecuniary norms of modern capitalism and the standards of engineering excellence, and he suggested that this conflict might become so great that engineers would possibly become a revolutionary group. Strauss does not believe that the professional-bureaucratic conflict is invested with such revolutionary implications, but he does suggest that

> there are conflicts between professional values and those of the organization.... In the first place, there are differences regarding objectives. The professionally oriented engineer is interested in doing meaningful work and in furthering his reputation in the profession; ... his professional pride is tied up with maintaining professional standards of excellence. The manager feels that the primary function of the engineer should be to develop products which can be sold at a profit; engineering standards are but a means to an end....
>
> The engineer is trained to think in terms of scientific logic ... As a consequence, he ... feels it unprofessional to compromise when he thinks he has the correct solution. The manager is used to dealing with intangibles and, to him, all questions involve shades of grey. He views the

engineer who refuses to compromise as an unrealistic prima donna....

Then there are major differences regarding the nature of authority. To the extent that the engineer is professionally oriented he feels that all questions should be open to free discussion by qualified professionals, with the final decision made on the basis of logical proof. His boss, he thinks, should be no more than a senior colleague who provides help when asked, but who does not give orders. ... The manager looks upon all this as sheer nonsense. From his point of view, status is based on position, not knowledge. The boss should make decisions and the subordinates should obey them without question (*218*, pp. 24–5).

Similar arguments have been advanced by writers such as Marcson (*156*), Kornhauser (*136*), and Scott (*200*).

The available empirical evidence indicates that the professional-bureaucratic conflict is not as pervasive as these writers suggest. Conflict between professional and organizational norms is not, as Hall (*98*; *99*) has shown, inherent in the relationship between professional employees and the organizations for which they work. This is not to deny that such conflict exists. Rather, it is to suggest that, as Hall, Ritti (*192*), and Cotgrove and Box (*22*; *39*) have demonstrated, the intensity of this conflict varies from one professional group to another, from one work context to another, and from one issue to another.

Leaving aside the debate about whether the 'professional ethic' produces conflict or harmony, there is some evidence from France which suggests that certain groups of professional technologists, often with managerial responsibilities and relatively high positions in the authority structure, do not accept the existing status structure in industry. Rather, they are impatient with the control of industry by a traditional and non-technical élite, and they feel that in determining the allocation of power and rewards criteria based upon technocratic achievement should replace the traditional criteria based primarily upon inherited wealth and social position. As Reynaud, in summing up the work of Maurice, Monteil, Guillon, and Gaulon (*162*), has pointed out:

> The leading claim of these employees is for increased participation in decision-making—within the enterprise but also in national economic affairs ... One finds mixed up within it the Christian affirmation of the responsibility that the most highly qualified must discharge within the community, appeals to technical or economic rationality made against traditional interests or the priority of financial considerations denunciations of capitalism and of profit-making, and semi-idyllic or at any rate idealised notions of the nature of American 'management' (*189*, pp. 153–4).

Thus without necessarily questioning the need for a higher managerial role, these employees are, contrary to what the status ideology would imply, challenging the legitimacy of many of the incumbents of managerial positions.

There are also other contexts in which professionals see relationships between themselves and other groups in terms of conflict. In fact, the very process of professionalization results in conflict between those groups which are generally recognized by society to be 'professional' and those which are not but would like to be. The reaction of doctors, particularly in the United States, to the professional claims of chiropractors and osteopaths is a case in point. Even within a single profession, conflicts over techniques, values, and goals may occur. Bucher and Strauss (*27*, pp. 325–6) note that many professionals are far from being united in their acceptance of the criteria of merit and the legitimacy of the status hierarchy prevailing within their profession. These differences of opinion tend to become 'patterned and shared' and 'coalitions develop and flourish'. For example, within the medical profession there is considerable disagreement between practitioners and researchers and between the members of one speciality and another as to which functions deserve the greater emphasis and status. Such disagreements involve definite conflicts of interest over the distribution of power, rewards, and facilities not only within the profession but also within the wider society.

There are at least two reasons why so many social scientists have failed to appreciate the conflict inherent in professionalism and professionalization. First, they have been led astray by certain professional associations which 'since they cherish and publish a common stereotype of themselves', to quote Hughes, 'engage in a common concealment'. The social scientist often becomes 'the dupe of this common concealment; the more so, since he, too, fancies himself a professional' (*114*, p. 425). Second, many social scientists have led themselves astray by tending to view society in structural-functionalist terms. Bucher and Strauss make this point very effectively:

> Functionalism sees a profession largely as a relatively homogeneous community whose members share identity, values, definitions of role, and interests. . . .
>
> But this kind of focus and theory tend to lead one to overlook many significant aspects of professions and professional life. Particularly does it bias the observer against appreciating the conflict—or at least difference—of interests within the profession; this leads him to overlook certain of the more subtle features of the profession's 'organization' as well as to fail to appreciate how consequential for changes in the profession and its practitioners differential interests may be (27, p. 325).

Collectivism. There is even less direct evidence of white-collar and professional workers' attitudes to collectivism than to conflict. But there is sufficient evidence to indicate that many of them see collectivism as appropriate at least in certain contexts. This would seem to be the case, for example, at the societal level in such fields as social welfare where collective action has replaced or supplemented individual provision. Runciman found in Britain that only 6 per cent of his total sample of both manual and white-collar workers were opposed to the general concept of the 'welfare state', and that the proportion of white-collar workers taking this view was only slightly higher than the proportion of manual workers. He also found that there was very little difference between the two groups on the questions of family allowances and unemployment benefit (*196*, pp. 22–6). Even in the United States where 'individualism' in the sphere of state welfare provision tends to be more entrenched than elsewhere, Hamilton found that 50 per cent of the clerical and sales workers in his sample were in favour of state action on unemployment and medical aid and that this proportion did not differ significantly from that among the skilled workers in the same sample (*100*, p. 194). The collective provision by the state of a basic minimum below which none shall fall does not, of course, preclude the possibility that some individuals, particularly at the higher occupational and income levels, may also make some additional private and individual provision in these spheres. But it does at least indicate that collectivism and individualism may coexist.

Collectivism is also seen as appropriate by some white-collar and professional workers in certain industrial contexts. In summarizing the results of some research in France (*162*), Reynaud has written:

A recent study—carried out among *cadres* in the French aircraft industry shows that while promotion and salaries remained, in their view, matters for individual bargaining, this was not the case with opportunities for further education and training which they regarded as matters to be discussed collectively (that is, as one appropriately handled by their unions) nor with questions of security of employment, in regard to which they felt that they should act jointly with other employees (*189*, p. 150).

In short, the selection of collective means or goals would seem to depend, at least to some extent, upon the issue concerned, and consequently there is not one type of orientation which is applied to all situations.

II. TRADE UNIONISM AND SOCIAL IMAGERY

The above evidence suggests that the class ideology is no monopoly of manual workers, nor the status ideology of white-collar workers. Many manual workers adhere to the values characteristic of the status ideology at least in certain contexts; similarly, many white-collar workers hold the values characteristic of the class ideology. In view of this, it is perhaps not surprising that many white-collar and manual workers view trade unions in a very similar way.

Images of Trade Unions

There has been a general tendency in the literature on the subject, as Chapter 1 made clear, to contrast the way in which white-collar and manual workers view unions. There are basically three propositions. First, since many more white-collar than manual workers have not joined unions, they are assumed to have a principled objection to them. Second, those white-collar workers who do join unions are assumed to be motivated primarily by instrumental considerations which are sufficiently strong to outweigh their principled objections, whereas manual workers are assumed to be motivated primarily by a principled commitment to unionism. Third, the white-collar unionists' instrumental motivation and the manual unionists' principled motivation are held to result in the former being less active and involved in union affairs than the latter. It will facilitate the discussion of these three propositions, if they are considered in reverse order.

Rawson has argued that manual unions expect and often obtain more 'ardent loyalty' from their members than white-collar unions do from theirs (*187*, p. 199). In the situations which Strauss observed, 'attendance at meetings and participation in union activities were generally lower on the part of white-collar workers than on the part of industrial workers' (*217*, p. 77). Routh has claimed that membership participation in white-collar unions is less than wholehearted; for most white-collar members 'the union plays a small part in their lives, they rarely if ever attend their branch meetings, they do not take the trouble to vote' (*195*, p. 201).

It is somewhat surprising that a low degree of membership participation should be singled out as a distinctive characteristic of white-collar unionists. For the 'apathy' of union members generally, whether white-collar or manual, has been repeatedly noted. To quote Spinrad:

> The lack of widespread membership participation in most trade unions, a counterpart of the similar phenomenon in other large-scale organizations, is a commonplace observation of both theorists and investigators (*215*, p. 237).

Moreover, Spinrad's survey of the literature reveals that

> Union activity is typically associated with a relatively 'higher' job. Thus, craft locals generally exhibit more participation than industrial locals. Among needle trades workers, the high status cutters and pressers participate more than do the others. Within industrial locals, the evidence is also striking that union activists, especially local leaders, except for the period of initial organization and during faction fights in some unions, are disproportionally drawn from those of relatively higher pay and job status (p. 239).

Similarly, Dufty found that a sample of white-collar

unionists in Australia had a slightly higher level of membership participation than a sample of skilled manual workers (55, p. 153–4). The available evidence is too scanty and unsystematic to allow the generalization that white-collar unionists are more active than manual unionists. But it supports even less the view that manual unionists have a higher degree of membership participation than white-collar unionists.

No one has studied membership participation in professional unions and associations in terms of such indices as attending meetings and voting in elections. Goldstein has argued, however, that because of the professional engineers' identification with the middle class ideal of self-sufficiency and individual initiative, they make less use of the grievance procedure than do manual workers (79, pp. 324–5).

But he cites very little empirical evidence, and none of a comparative nature, to support his contention. Moreover, even granted that professionals do file relatively fewer grievances, it does not necessarily follow that they are less active or less committed trade unionists as Goldstein implies. They may simply have fewer grievances perhaps because employers are more considerate of their interests and aspirations than of those of manual workers. Finally, even granted that professionals have as many grievances as manual workers, it does not necessarily follow that 'some subconscious feeling of shame attached to union membership' prevents them from using the grievance procedure. They may simply be able to handle their grievances more effectively outside the scope of the formal procedure perhaps because their employment situation is not as bureaucratized as that of manual workers.

Even if it could be demonstrated that white-collar and professional unionists were less active and involved in union affairs than manual unionists, it would not necessarily follow that this was because the former had an instrumental attachment to unionism whereas the latter had a principled commitment. For the extent to which union members are active is often determined not by their attitudes to unionism, but by such structural factors as the size of the branch and whether it is organized on the place of work or on a geographical basis.

But even granted that white-collar workers have an instrumental orientation towards their unions, this does not make them unique. For a common view of unionism, amongst both white-collar and manual workers, would seem to be instrumental rather than principled. For example, Goldthorpe and his colleagues found that union membership had little meaning for most of their 'affluent' manual workers other than in relation to the immediate 'bread-and-butter' issues of their own work situation. They note that

> Taking an overall view, ... it may be said that not only have a substantial number of our affluent workers been brought into the trade union movement only in the course of their present employment, but also that no more than a small minority appear to have been in any way motivated in this respect through moral conviction. More frequently, these men would seem to have become union-ists either with little volition on their own part or because of a belief—often expressed to us—that 'union member-ship pays'; that is, as a result of a largely instrumental view of unionism which clearly reflects what we would regard as their characterstic orientation towards their working life in general (*86*, p. 98).

They feel that this instrumental orientation towards unions distinguishes their 'affluent workers' from other manual workers. They recognize that

> all trade unionism, like all work activity, contains a basically instrumental component. Nonetheless, unionism has often represented *more* to workers than simply a means of economic betterment; it has been seen also as

a form of collective action in which solidarity was an end as well as a means and as a socio-political movement aiming at radical changes in industrial institutions and in the structure of society generally. In our view, the most distinctive feature of the unionism of the workers we studied is the *extent* to which these wider ideals and objectives have ceased to be of significance (pp. 107-8).

It is very debatable, however, to what extent the attitudes of affluent workers differ from those of other manual workers. The comparative material presented by Goldthorpe and his colleagues is, as Woodward has argued, 'not substantial and the impression is given that the comparisons are based on what traditional workers' attitudes might be expected to be' (*247*, p. 132). That an instrumental view of unions is more widespread than Goldthorpe and his colleagues think is borne out, for example, by McKenzie and Silver's findings from a large-scale survey of manual workers generally that

> For all but a few working class people unions appear to be valued only for their specific bargaining functions. The admission, grudging or enthusiastic that they are indispensable for this purpose is typically followed by some form of criticism suggesting unions are useful instruments rather than cherished objects of loyalty.

> .   .   .

> Thus, unions are widely seen as necessary agencies of defense, rather infrequently praised with basic enthusiasm, and often criticised for a variety of alleged faults and failings. Agreement with the unions' goal of improving the lot of ordinary people very often does not involve a thoroughgoing approval of unions as institutions or political organisations (*165*, pp. 130, 133).

The extent to which trade unionists support the link between the trade union movement and the Labour Party is often taken as a more specific index of the degree to which they have a principled belief in unionism.

Chapter 3 demonstrated that this link is prompted at least partly by considerations of an instrumental nature and hence cannot easily be used for this purpose. But even granting for a moment that it could, there is evidence which indicates that the link between the trade unions and the Labour Party is viewed with a lack of enthusiasm, if not suspicion and hostility, not only by white-collar unionists but also by many manual unionists.

Goldthorpe and his colleagues found (*86*, pp. 109–12) that although most of their affluent workers were Labour voters, a majority of them thought that trade unions and the Labour Party should keep themselves separate. Even taking only those workers who were Labour supporters, they found that among the setters and semi-skilled men still only 51 per cent favoured the unions' close association with the Labour Party. Even among the craftsmen who were Labour supporters, only 68 per cent favoured the political link. They also found that 25 per cent of the sample had contracted out of paying the political levy and that in all groups except the craftsmen from a third to a half were making their contribution without being aware that they were doing so. In fact, it was only among the craftsmen that a majority of the unionists paid the political levy and were aware that they did; for the other groups this figure was only about 40 per cent. On the basis of this evidence, Goldthorpe and his colleagues concluded that

> it would appear, first, that in the consciousness of many of our affluent workers the political involvement of their union is not a matter of any great saliency; and, secondly, that of those who are more politically aware, a sizeable number are not prepared to support their union in its affiliation to the Labour Party. In sum, it is fairly clearly indicated that these workers are not to any large degree committed to the traditional idea of the trade unions and the Labour Party as forming the industrial and

political 'wings' of an integrated labour movement (p. 111).

Nor are such political attitudes restricted to affluent manual workers. McKenzie and Silver found that among the trade unionists in their national sample of manual workers, 7 per cent had contracted out, 23 per cent actually voted Conservative in spite of paying the levy, and none of the remaining 70 per cent regarded themselves as individually committed to the Labour Party by paying the levy (*165*, p. 99). Drawing on evidence from repeated interviews with a nationwide sample of the electorate, Butler and Stokes found that only 25 to 31 per cent of union members thought that trade unions should have close ties to the Labour Party (*30*, p. 169). A national Gallup Poll in 1964 demonstrated that 37 per cent of trade unionists (as compared to 43 per cent of non-unionists) felt it was a 'bad thing' that the trade union movement was so closely linked to the Labour Party (*71*). Hill found that even a majority of his sample of London dockers objected to the alliance between unionism and the Labour Party (*105*, p. 340). Similar evidence comes from Australia where Dufty found that among his samples of manual and white-collar railway unionists, the former were more critical of the link between the trade unions and the Australian Labour Party than the latter (*55*, pp. 155–6).

This indifference and opposition to political activity is confirmed by more detailed studies of particular unions. In spite of the draughtsmen's union being very militant industrially, 60 per cent of its members contract out of paying the political levy for the Labour Party (*8*, p. 118). The membership of the industrially militant Scottish Typographical Association has been balloted on eight occasions since World War I as to whether or not a political fund should be established, and on each occasion the vote has been in the negative. Before and during one of these ballots in 1954, Sykes interviewed

84 of the Association's Glasgow members. Although 69 of them voted for the Labour Party, only 18 were in favour of their union establishing a political fund. The remainder were opposed. Their reasons were highly instrumental in nature:

> The general feeling among those interviewed was that the trade union should not get involved in politics. The reason generally given being that if it did politics would become dominant and the trade union aspect would suffer. In particular it was said that officials had to be 'kept in hand', they would like to 'play at politics' and if they were allowed to do so their union would suffer (*224*, p. 178).

Similarly, a study of a large local union of steel workers in the United States by Seidman, London, and Karsh revealed that

> Whereas all the leaders and active members interviewed agreed that the union should be active politically, only about half of the inactives shared such views, and then mostly with reservations as to the type of activity that should be undertaken or the issues that should be acted on. Fully a fourth of the inactives opposed union political action, usually on the ground that the union's proper interests were limited to collective bargaining (*203*, p. 699).

Even active manual unionists are not always in favour of political action by their unions. Sykes noted that some of the active and militant members of the Scottish Typographical Association felt that 'from a purely trade union point of view, it was better to keep politics out of the union' (*224*, p. 178). And a study of shipbuilding workers in Tyneside revealed that twice as many shop stewards voted Conservative in 1966 as shipyard workers (17 per cent compared to 9 per cent); fewer of the stewards paid the political levy (64 per cent compared to 71 per cent); far more of the stewards were able to state that they had definitely contracted out (36 per cent compared to 18 per cent); and about 50 per cent of both stewards and workers thought that the connection between the unions and the Labour Party should not be maintained (*41*, p. 226).

Thus there is evidence which indicates that relatively few manual workers have a principled commitment to unionism. Many, if not most, appear to see unionism in purely instrumental terms. In any case, no simple contrast can be drawn between white-collar and manual unionists' images of trade unions. For these are at least partly dependent upon factors, such as the degree of organization of the workplace and the compliance structure of the union, which are not exclusive to either white-collar or manual workers.

The question of union membership is rarely a completely voluntary decision. In highly unionized workplaces, indifferent or unwilling employees may be subjected to such negative sanctions as social pressure and ostracism and, where the closed shop exists, the threat of dismissal. Even where membership is essentially 'voluntary', employees may be subjected to such positive sanctions as friendly benefits and discount schemes. In these situations, the decision to join is generally going to be essentially instrumental in nature. Probably only in deciding to join a union in predominantly non-union situations, where in the absence of recognition for collective bargaining little direct economic pay-off can be expected, is the decision to join generally going to indicate a principled commitment to unionism.*

Even in these situations, however, it does not necessarily follow that those white-collar (and manual)

---

* For example, Butler and Stokes found that 87 per cent of union members in the least unionized workplaces support the Labour Party compared to 54 per cent in the fully (but not compulsorily) unionized workplaces, the latter figure being little different from that for non-unionists (*30*, p. 159).

workers who do not join unions have a principled objection to them. Those who argue that unions are opposed
for principled reasons and accepted for instrumental
reasons are posing an asymmetrical argument which
omits the other two logical possibilities: that workers
accept unions for principled reasons, and that they reject
them for instrumental reasons.

There is some evidence which suggests that this latter
possibility occurs fairly frequently. The Opinion Research Corporation has conducted several large-scale
surveys of white-collar opinion in the United States.
All of them have revealed that at least as many white-
collar workers wanted to join unions as were already
members of them, and that less than 50 per cent of each
sample was definitely opposed to joining unions (cited
by Lipset, *147*, pp. 57–8). Kuhn has pointed out that an
examination of the 'work scene and conditions of
employment' of many American professional engineers
reveals a lack of bureaucratization with the result that
there is 'ample opportunity for individual bargaining'
and 'little to encourage engineers to organize for *collective bargaining*' (*137*, p. 194). Kuhn's argument is
confirmed by Riegel's study of the attitudes of unorganized engineers and scientists in the United States.
Although a majority of his sample were opposed to the
idea of collective bargaining, this was primarily for
instrumental reasons: over a third said that they were
in a strong market situation at the moment and therefore did not need a union to add strength to their
bargaining position, and a further group thought that
their jobs were not sufficiently standardized to make
collective bargaining a practical proposition (*191*, pp.
42–70). The absence of unionization among white-collar
workers in the United States, as Taylor has noted,

> is somewhat myopically viewed as opposition to unioniza-
> tion. In fact, a more discerning analysis warrants a con-
> clusion that the professions and white-collar occupations

rather than being against unionization have little need of unionization (*228*, p. 160).

Even in Britain where the degree of white-collar unionization is much higher than in the United States, a survey of white-collar workers by Mercer and Weir revealed that those who objected to trade unionism did so on many grounds, but within each occupational group the predominant reason was 'we don't need one' (*167*, p. 58).

Rather than indicating that white-collar workers have a principled objection to unionism, the absence of union membership among them may simply indicate that they have never considered the question. As C. Wright Mills has noted,

> For most white-collar employees to join or not to join a union has never been a live question, for no union has been available, or, if it has, was not energetically urging affiliation. For these employees, the question has been to organize or not to organize a union, which is a very different proposition from joining or not joining an available union (*169*, p. 306).

This statement is supported by the Opinion Research Corporation study referred to above which revealed that over the years 1945 to 1957 when the surveys were conducted, between 60 and 71 per cent of those interviewed stated that they did not know of any recruiting efforts in the place in which they worked (cited by Lipset, *147*, p. 59). It might be argued that they were not sufficiently pro-union to organize a branch or to become individual members without being approached. But in this respect they differ little from manual workers. For, as Lipset has pointed out, 'few workers, manual or non-manual, take active steps to join unions which are not actively trying to organize the company in which they work' (p. 59).

Trade Unionists and Class Consciousness

Regardless of whether white-collar or manual unionists view their unions in instrumental or principled terms, the question still remains as to what extent these views reflect a wider class consciousness. Writers such as Lockwood and Blackburn have tried to show that union members are class conscious by pointing to such behavioural aspects of trade unionism as strikes and affiliation to the T.U.C. and the Labour Party. The fundamental weakness of such an approach is the methodology employed. Union behaviour is often determined, as Chapter 3 made clear, not so much by the attitudes of union members as by structural factors external to them. This means that the attitudes of members need not necessarily be congruent with union behaviour, and hence it is not possible to derive conclusions about the former simply by observing the latter. Indeed, if this were possible, then a good deal of the evidence about union behaviour assembled in Chapter 3 would suggest that trade unionists are not class conscious. There is, however, another way of demonstrating that trade unionists are class conscious, and that is to subject them to interview or questionnaire techniques and thereby produce direct evidence of such an ideology.

Prandy is one of the few writers who has attempted to do this in any systematic fashion. He argues, as Chapter 1 indicated, that the existence of a trade union reveals 'a major break from normal, accepted middle-class values'. For by bargaining with employers on behalf of employees and thereby giving expression to a conflict of interest, a trade union is a 'class association' whose members recognize that they have common interests which conflict with those of employers. He therefore takes the existence of a trade union as 'an indication of class attitudes' (*184*, pp. 42–3). By contrast he takes the existence of a professional association as an indication of status attitudes. For although he admits that many of the activities of trade unions and professional associations 'are very similar, and are mainly directed to the same end of economic protection', he argues that 'it is important to realize the differences in ideology which underlie the two'. In short, 'trade unions are class bodies—they bargain with employers; professional associations are status bodies—they bestow a qualification and seek to maintain or enhance its prestige' (pp. 43–4).

In an attempt to prove his argument, Prandy examined two professional associations—the Institution of Metallurgists and the Engineers' Guild—and a trade union—the Association of Scientific Workers. He sent a postal questionnaire to a sample of the members of the Institution of Metallurgists and found (pp. 87–105) that the desire to obtain a qualification was given by over 62 per cent as their reason for joining, that 48 per cent believed the Institution's main function to be the conduct of examinations, that 52 per cent wanted the Institution to do more to improve the use made of their professional knowledge, and that 54 per cent thought the Institution should concern itself more with raising their status. But he also found that 47 per cent wanted the Institution to concern itself more with raising their salaries, a view which Prandy feels is likely to lead to activities of a class type. He points out, however, that most respondents wanted the Institution to do this not by collective bargaining or unilateral regulation but by publicity and education. Prandy concluded from these findings that

> The main emphasis of these professional people is clearly on status, which is most influential in determining their opinions. Nevertheless, there are tendencies towards class attitudes amongst certain groups, especially those who want the Institution to engage in more activities concerned with the protective function (p. 105).

He then interviewed members of the Engineers' Guild in the Merseyside area, and found (pp. 111–21) that a desire for a body to deal with salaries or 'a bargaining body' was as common a reason for joining as 'a desire to improve the status of engineers'; that although raising the status of the engineering profession was the most common view of the Guild's function, dealing with salaries was the second most common view; that almost as many respondents thought the Guild should concern itself more with salaries as with status; and that almost half were in favour of collective bargaining, and those who were not generally objected for practical rather than principled reasons. He concluded that

> Obviously many Guild members are concerned with status, and a status ideology has a good deal of influence on their attitudes. Nevertheless, there are almost as many who lean further towards class ideas, represented by those who joined because they wanted the Guild to deal with salaries, or because they wanted it to be a bargaining body (p. 112).

Finally, Prandy interviewed members of the A.Sc.W. living in the Merseyside area and found (pp. 157–70) that most joined for such reasons as the need for representation on salaries and conditions of work or because of threatened redundancy, that most saw the improvement of salaries and conditions as being the main function of the A.Sc.W., that three-quarters of the respondents had a favourable attitude towards collective bargaining, and that about half felt that trade unionism and politics were necessarily connected although only a minority saw the connection in terms of the Labour Party. He concluded that although A.Sc.W. members tend to have a class ideology, 'the influence of status ideas is still strong, even within a class organization' (p. 170).

These findings do not demonstrate any clear-cut connection between trade unions and a class ideology or between professional associations and a status ideology. Rather, they reveal a 'confusion of ideologies' with considerable status elements among trade union members and considerable class elements among professional association members. Clearly, such a confusion of ideologies does not provide a basis for classifying trade unions as class bodies and professional associations as status bodies. In short, the evidence from Prandy's questionnaires and interviews does not support his argument.

But even if Prandy's empirical findings did support his argument, they could not be taken at their face value. For his analysis is characterized by several methodological problems. To begin with, his samples are small and, with the possible exception of the postal questionnaire administered to the members of the Institution of Metallurgists, somewhat unrepresentative. In addition, the questionnaires and interview schedules are not well suited to the theoretical framework. The latter rests upon Weber's distinction between class and status, but the questions put are neither phrased nor answered in Weberian terms. Consequently, what people say has to be translated out of their words and into the very categories which they are supposed to be assessing. For example, some of Prandy's respondents claimed that they joined the Engineers' Guild because they thought it was 'a good idea'. Prandy claims that this sort of reason is 'associated' with a status ideology (pp. 180–1). It may be. But the sentiment that the Guild is 'a good idea' is so vague that it might well be associated with almost anything. Clearly, when the research design allows this much scope for ambiguity and arbitrary variation in classification, it does not provide an adequate basis upon which to gauge people's social imagery.

Prandy's failure to demonstrate that trade unionists are class conscious does not, of course, prove that they are not. But there is other evidence which suggests that trade unionists do not necessarily have a class ideology, and that, as a corollary, a status ideology is not necessarily inimical to unionism. In fact, a good deal of the evidence presented in the first section of this chapter has already done this. For many of the manual workers who were shown there to possess elements of a status ideology were trade unionists. There are also two other pieces of evidence which are worth presenting.

Recent studies reveal that the views of trade unionists on the position of unions in the wider society are often very critical. Goldthorpe and his colleagues found that over 40 per cent of their affluent workers felt that 'trade unions have too much power in the country' (*86*, pp. 112–13). Even a majority of Hill's sample of dockers felt that unions had too much power in society (*105*, p. 340). Similarly, Butler and Stokes found that almost 50 per cent of their respondents from union households felt that unions had too much power, and that even 31 per cent of union members who voted Labour in 1964 took this view. When asked whether their sympathies were generally for or against strikers, 45 per cent of the respondents from union families said, 'against' (*30*, pp. 167–8). Thus rather than contributing to a broader class consciousness, the trade unionists' role as union member would often seem to be segregated or compartmentalized from other roles which they play in society.

This compartmentalization can exist even within the relatively homogeneous environment of the workplace. As Stagner has pointed out:

> The armchair theorist would have it that the worker must choose one organization and reject the other. Either he should try to maximize personal advantage by rising within the company, or he should follow group interest and identify with the union.... But as soon as investigators began to explore the problem at its proper level— in the rank and file of the mass-production factory— it became clear that the theory of unilateral loyalty had to be replaced by a more complex formulation taking

account of the phenomena of overlapping membership and multiple allegiances (*216*, p. viii).

This statement is supported by a number of research studies (*53*; *186*; *193*) which suggest that it is possible, perhaps even normal, for workers at any point of time to demonstrate 'dual loyalty'. Rose's conclusion is typical:

> People can have loyalty to two (or more) groups or two sets of values, even when those groups or values are in conflict. In concrete terms, loyalty to the union does not mean disloyalty to the employer (*193*, p. 189).

In other words, there is no reason why 'in any particular situation, one would expect there to be a tendency for an individual's views to be either predominantly of a class or a status type', as Prandy assumes (*184*, p. 38).

Clearly, this evidence is fragmentary and hardly proves that trade unionists do not generally adhere to a class ideology. It is, therefore, worth considering whether it would be possible to evolve a research design that could adequately demonstrate that trade unions are class bodies and professional associations are status bodies. It might be possible, but such a research design would certainly face a number of conceptual and operational problems.

The first operational problem concerns the indicators to be used to distinguish those respondents holding a class ideology from those holding a status ideology. Prandy, for example, assumes that respondents who want more done about salaries have a class ideology and that those who want more done about status have a status ideology. Such an interpretation is not necessarily warranted. Salary is often taken as an index of status. The result is that the two concepts are inextricably intertwined in many people's minds, and when they refer to salary, they may mean status, and when they refer to status, they may mean salary. Even if it is

salary rather than status to which they are referring,
it is not immediately obvious why this is indicative of
a class ideology. The desire for higher incomes is sufficiently widespread that it is almost certainly not restricted to those with a class ideology. And even if it
is status rather than salary to which people are referring, it is most doubtful if they are defining 'status' in
the same way as the sociological literature. There is a
fairly good chance that they are simply implying that
they would like more recognition and respect for the
role they perform in society. This is quite different from
the conception of status as a harmonious view of society
which legitimizes the power of the ruling class.

Even if adequate indicators of class and status ideologies could be located, there would still be the problem
of dual members and non-members. Several studies
(*133; 202*) have shown that many professional employees
see no contradiction in belonging to both a professional
association and a trade union, and it is well known that
some of them are members of both types of organizations
(*184*, p. 121). Do dual members hold a single social
image and, if so, is it a class or a status ideology? Regardless of which ideology they hold, how does it lead them
to join both a trade union and a professional association? Alternatively, do dual members hold different
social images in different social contexts? That is, do
they hold a status ideology in some contexts which leads
them to join a professional association and a class ideology in other contexts which leads them also to join a
trade union, and, if so, what accounts for this dual
imagery.* And what about non-members? Do they hold

---

* The existence of dual members or prospective dual members also
makes it difficult to interpret the respondents' replies. For when
dual members of a professional association state that they do not
want it to engage in collective bargaining, this does not necessarily
mean that they are opposed to collective bargaining in principle.
Rather, they might simply be implying that another body of which
they are or would like to be members should perform this function.

a class or a status ideology? If they do hold one of these images, why does it not lead them to join a trade union or a professional association? Alternatively, do non-members adhere to a third type of image, and, if so, what is its nature?

Most important, there are fundamental conceptual difficulties with the distinction often made between 'class' and 'status'. Prandy's work is a case in point. He claims that 'class relationships are inherently ones of conflict, for the interests of the two groups are opposed and incompatible', and that such a relationship is 'qualitatively different' from status relationships which are 'essentially harmonious' (pp. 33, 37). Such a sharp contrast is not warranted. To begin with, as Prandy himself points out, the 'status system is created out of the class system by the attempt of the superordinate group to have their power legitimized' (p. 39), and 'it is most important to realize that these two forms of stratification are analytically distinct, if only because in practice they are inextricably confused' (p. 174).

Moreover, it is debatable if 'class' and 'status' are even as 'analytically distinct' as Prandy assumes. For status stratification need not necessarily be harmonious. Prandy admits that there may be 'competition' between individuals to raise their status, but he argues that 'the validity of the criteria by which status is measured, the bases of legitimation, is not questioned' (p. 37). But surely individuals and groups may hold a status ideology in the sense that they see the social structure as being completely open, with a hierarchy of strata which can be scaled on the basis of individual merit, but never-

---

For example, at the end of 1954 the Royal Institute of British Architects sent a questionnaire to all architects which included the question: 'Are you in favour of having a trade union composed wholly or mainly of architects and approved by the R.I.B.A., and would you join?' Of those who replied, 63 per cent, or nearly 6,000, did so in the affirmative, and only about 2,400 of these were already members of a trade union (cited by Grant, *91*, p. 128).

theless perceive themselves to be in conflict with other individuals and groups because they disagree as to the criteria by which status should be measured. As John Rex has argued:

> It is an obvious fact of our experience that where birth is claimed as a criterion of status it is challenged by those who wish to replace it by money, education, occupation or social function. And each of these would be challenged by all the others....
>
> Clearly the best that can be said is that the case in which there is unanimity on status valuations is a limiting one rarely, if ever, found empirically. The usual case is that in which there is considerable conflict as to what the criterion of status should be.... Thus it would be true to say that a conflict of status ideologies is an essential part of all status-class relations (*188*, pp. 147–8).

Similarly, those who see society in terms of two major classes need not necessarily see the relationship between them in terms of conflict. They may see it in terms of either benevolent dependence or functional interdependence.*

Regardless of how distinct 'class' and 'status' are, they do not coincide clearly and exclusively with either 'collective bargaining' or the 'qualifying function'. Rather, the latter concepts each embody by their very nature both class and status elements. Prandy claims collective bargaining is a class activity since it gives expression to a conflict of interest between employer and employee. But, as Chapter 3 has already demonstrated, this is a somewhat one-sided view. For while collective bargaining obviously does give expression to a conflict of interest between employer and employee, it just as obviously gives recognition to their common interests by regulating and institutionalizing this conflict. In Dahrendorf's words,

---

* This point is developed more fully *infra*, p. 150.

the essential fact is that by collective bargaining the frozen fronts of industrial conflict are thawed. If the representatives of management and labor meet regularly for negotiations, gradual changes of social structure replace the tendency toward revolutionary explosions and civil war (*47*, p. 260).

Moreover, collective bargaining does not involve a rejection of the employer's legitimacy. A prerequisite for collective bargaining is 'mutual recognition', a recognition by each party of the legitimacy of the other. As Hyman has noted:

while collective bargaining has eliminated some of the more glaringly brutal accoutrements of managerial control, it has consolidated the basic structure. The legitimation which trade unionism accords to management—for in collective bargaining, the obverse of employer recognition of the union is union recognition of the employer —is particularly welcome, simply because workers' organisations might otherwise act as vehicles of oppositional ideology (*118*, p. 96).

Similarly, the qualifying function also embodies both class and status elements. Prandy suggests that the qualifying function is 'clearly related to the idea of status, since the reason for controlling the quality of members is to maintain or enhance the status of the whole group, assuming that ability will be given due financial and other rewards' (*184*, p. 123). This is true. But it is equally true, as the quotation from Prandy implies, that the qualifying function is closely related to the question of improving salaries, an activity which he feels is primarily connected with a class ideology and trade unionism. For status is sought after not only for its intrinsic value but also because of its instrumental value. As Wootton has perceptively noted:

Skilful manipulation of the mutual interaction of pay, prestige and professional competence is indeed one of the remarkable achievements of our age, which is distinguished for its pride in professionalism. Status, remuneration and training or professional skill are constantly discussed together; and by a subtle blending of these elements, money is made to appear a measure of virtue.... Status depends on pay: and pay and status together are presented as the guarantees not only of professional competence, but also of integrity, and indeed of every other virtue, as one occupation after another turns to good account methods originally devised by unions of manual workers to protect themselves against rapacious employers (*248*, p. 184).

Even more important, the qualifying function implies collectivism and conflict as much as individualism and harmony. For as this chapter has already indicated (*supra*, pp. 123–4), the maintenance of standards and the control of entry which this implies is primarily a collective goal which by its very nature can only be pursued collectively and which almost inevitably involves conflict with other groups and interests.

Ultimately, the literature seeking to distinguish class and status ideologies, and to connect these to trade unions and to professional associations, must face the problem of specifying adequately the nature of class consciousness. Yet, as was clear in the earlier discussion of union character, this has still to be done. For Prandy, class consciousness is taken to involve 'a consciousness of the class system', that is a 'consciousness of conflict of interest' which 'in practice can be more or less intense' and vary from ' "individual" to "group" and finally "class" consciousness' (*184*, pp. 38, 42–3). Such a specification of class consciousness hardly illuminates the theoretical problems associated with the concept. 'Class' consciousness can hardly be 'individual' consciousness unless it is argued that the individual is coterminous with a class. Similarly, whether 'group' consciousness is also 'class' consciousness will depend upon whether 'group' is defined widely enough and 'class' narrowly enough for the two concepts to coincide. Prandy does not delimit the scope of a 'group' or a 'class', but he clearly sees a difference between the two concepts. For he points out that 'how far even many groups of manual workers, including trade unionists, can be said to exhibit this last type ['class' as opposed to 'individual' or 'group' consciousness] is surely open to question' (p. 43). Indeed, it is. Hence even if Prandy's analysis were valid, he would have only demonstrated that his trade unionists had, at best, a 'group' consciousness. His fundamental error is in recognizing that Lockwood's distinction between group and class consciousness 'is a valid point, but should not be overstressed' (p. 42). Perhaps it should not, but neither should it be ignored. For if it is, the debate as to whether or not trade unionists are class conscious is lost by default.

III. CONCLUSION

This chapter has demonstrated that white-collar and manual workers cannot be polarized in terms of their images of society, industry, or trade unions. It has also shown that a class ideology is neither a necessary prerequisite for nor consequence of trade union membership among either white-collar or manual workers, and, as a corollary, that a status ideology is not necessarily inimical to unionism. This does not mean, however, that workers' social imagery or ideologies have no impact on trade unionism. For the critique presented in this chapter has had to stay within the frame of reference of those who have posed the class and status ideologies, and these concepts are far too holistic and rigid to encompass usefully the variety of images current in a complex and dynamic industrial society.

Indeed, some stratification theorists have modified the original class-status dichotomy in the belief that it does not encompass the full range of social imagery.

Even Prandy who is at some pains to maintain the dichotomous model, points out that the class and status ideologies are ideal types which form the poles of a continuum of images, and that certain groups in the middle of the social hierarchy may possess a mixture of ideologies (*184*, pp. 38, 174). Lockwood, in his work with Goldthorpe and others, has drawn attention to three different types of manual workers who hold three different types of images. They are:

> first, the traditional worker of the 'proletarian' variety whose image of society will take the form of a power model; secondly, the other variety of traditional worker, the 'deferential', whose perception of social inequality will be one of status hierarchy; and thirdly, the 'privatised' worker, whose social consciousness will most nearly approximate what may be called a 'pecuniary' model of society (*152*, p. 250).

The pecuniary model of society is the social image associated with the orientation which Goldthorpe and Lockwood call 'instrumental collectivism'. This combines the individual ends of the status ideology with the collective means of the class ideology (*84*, pp. 153–4). But even the addition of this third image does not exhaust all the possible images of society, and hence the resulting typology is still too simple to embrace the complexities of the phenomena which it seeks to describe.

The formulation of this third image by Goldthorpe and Lockwood recognizes that two of the elements of social imagery outlined in Table I (*supra*, p. 14)—modes of mobility and the relationship between ends and means—permit more possibilities than those envisaged by the class and status ideologies. That is, collective goals and collective ascent through the stratification system can be combined with the notion of individual means to individual ascent to produce a 'hybrid' in which individual goals may be pursued by collective means. What it fails to recognize is that the remaining elements of social imagery—the mode of stratification and the relationship between classes or categories—also permit many more possibilities than those envisaged by the class and status ideologies.*

In terms of the mode of stratification, there is the basic distinction between those who perceive the social structure as comprising interacting social classes with differential power, and those who see it in terms of a hierarchy of descriptive social categories placed in order according to various criteria of prestige. In the class ideology model there are only two classes, and in the status ideology model there are an infinite number of finely graded hierarchical categories. But in both cases the number of classes or groups could obviously be varied: there could be more than two conflicting classes, and there could also be a limited number of hierarchical categories.

The class and status ideology models used in the literature on trade unionism allow only for conflict between classes and harmony between social categories. But again there are many more possibilities. Those who see society in terms of Capital and Labour or Rulers and Ruled do not necessarily perceive the relationship between these classes in terms of conflict. Some may see it in terms of benevolent dependence or functional interdependence. And some may see strong cultural barriers between the two classes 'us' and 'them', but perceive this distinction not in terms of conflict but simply as a question of separateness of identity and behaviour.

Similarly, there can be conflict as well as consensus over the distribution of prestige. For prestige is not only a reward based on a consensual estimation of honour, it is also a facility which enables a group to improve its

* For an excellent discussion of the complexities of social imagery see Ossowski (*173*).

own life chances relative to other groups. Prestige can be used, as Eisenstadt has pointed out,

> as a basis for getting other commodities—such as money or power, or services. True enough, prestige is not usually directly interchangeable for power or money; very often any attempt to use prestige in such a way would entail its loss. But those having prestige can often use it as starting points for specially favourable bargaining positions, for the acquisition of other types of services, commodities or media of exchange. . . . Moreover, prestige —the right of participation in different collectivities, socio-cultural orders and centres—can also be used to assure one's access to other institutional positions, such as economic or power ones, and to attempt to limit the possibilities of other people having such access (*61*, p. 70).

Hence there can obviously be disagreement over prestige rankings which may in some cases lead to conflict between social groups.

A further problem with the class and status dichotomy is that it tends to assume that individuals perceive the social structure in holistic terms: that all relationships in industry and the wider society will be seen in terms of conflict and collectivism or harmony and individualism. But various aspects of the class and status ideologies need not necessarily coalesce. Conflict in one sphere may coexist with consensus in another. For example, consensus over the general distribution of power in society may coexist with conflict over the allocation of power in the workplace. Even within the workplace, consensus over the goals of the company may coexist with conflict over the distribution of rewards within it. Moreover, to present the company as divided into two sets of coherent reference groups—management and union or management and the employees—rather than in terms of a multiplicity of reference groups and relationships is misleading. Not only are there a variety of relationships with management, but there are also a number of different sources of allegiance among employees, especially where the labour force is highly differentiated by skill and function. For example, work groups may combine to fight the employer over redundancy but find themselves in conflict with each other over demarcation of work or wage differentials. Indeed, one group may even ally itself with the employer in order to defeat the other. In short, the degree to which the orientations in these various contexts are superimposed upon one another to form a single all embracing *weltanschaung* can not be determined by *a priori* reasoning but only by empirical investigation.

Thus the analysis of attitudes needs to be multi-dimensional, allowing for all the possible permutations and combinations of the elements of social imagery and for the variety of contexts in which perceptions are formed. If such an analysis were undertaken and if the behavioural consequences of the different images were more clearly and effectively demonstrated, then the attempt to link social structure to unionization by means of social imagery might be more successful.

5

Conclusions

This study has focused on the literature concerned with
the interplay of social stratification and trade unionism.
This literature, as should now be clear, varies enor-
mously in its sophistication. At its crudest, the argument is simply that union growth and character are
correlated with various indices of position in the social
stratification system, and that these correlations are
prima facie evidence for the existence of a causal link
between stratification and unionization. More refined
variants do not challenge this basic assumption of a
causal relationship. Rather, their refinements take a
number of forms. Some polarize types of employee
organizations in order to isolate more precisely the
impact of stratification on union growth and character.
Others break away from this polarization to argue that
position in a highly differentiated stratification system
only generates a continuum of organizational behaviour.
And still others explain the apparent correlation between stratification and unionism by specifying the
intervening role of the social images generated by differing class and status positions. But however refined the
argument, the common assumption remains that union
growth and character in modern industrial societies are
best explained by reference to the twin categories of
class and status. On the precise definition and significance of class and status, the literature shows only ambiguity, disagreement, and downright confusion. But
on the importance of these categories for unionism it

demonstrates a rare and impressive unity.

All this the study has considered and challenged. In Chapter 2 the interconnections between social stratification and union growth were subjected to close scrutiny. It was shown that, no matter how wide and various were the definitions of social position, there was no easy correlation between them and patterns of union growth.

In Chapter 3 it was shown that there is no close and simple relationship between the social position of an organization's membership and that organization's goals or behaviour. Different social positions do not generate or sustain distinct organizational types. Nor can the character of an organization be taken as an adequate measure of the class or trade union consciousness of its membership. For the concepts of character and consciousness are more complex than the literature suggests, and the relationship between them is too tenuous to permit one to be taken as a measure of the other.

Finally, it was suggested in Chapter 4 that one reason for the literature's misspecification of the relationship between unionism and stratification lay in its inadequate treatment of the nature of social imagery. Far from distinct class or status positions generating simple, coherent, and distinct images of social reality which then shape and sustain markedly different patterns of union growth and character, perceptions of reality were demonstrated to be varied, overlapping, and capable of change over time. No easy equation could then reasonably be expected between social position, social imagery, and trade unionism.

It might be argued, however, that certain limitations of the data and method employed here seriously undermine the strength of the argument offered. To begin with, it might be objected that there is too heavy a reliance upon data which have often been gathered for other purposes and which were intended to answer questions that do not always conform exactly to those of concern to this study. There is certainly a reliance on such data, but it is unavoidable. For the theories which have been discussed here cover a large number of occupations, industries, and countries. It would be difficult, not to say impossible, to undertake new work in all these areas in order to assess them. In any case, there is sufficient data available to establish the inadequacies of the theories surveyed. Indeed, the study has often done little more than bring the theories on unionism and stratification face-to-face with the evidence which their proponents should themselves have considered or which has become available only after the theories were advanced.

It might also be argued that the study merely identifies the 'exceptions which prove the rule'. The notion that rules are proved by the exceptions which refute them is a convenient philosophy for those who generalize on insufficient or inadequate evidence. In any case, the study has been considering arguments of a general kind which suggest that certain aspects of unionism can best be explained by social stratification variables. Hence it becomes legitimate to indicate those situations in which these aspects of unionism cannot be so explained. Moreover, these situations are far too numerous to be dismissed as aberrations from a more general trend. Rather, they are the very core evidence with which the literature on social stratification and unionism has to come to terms.

None the less, it is neither possible nor desirable to dismiss completely the impact of social stratification upon union growth and character. Analysis can take place at many levels, and this study has concentrated, as did the literature it surveyed, on highly aggregative patterns of union growth and character. The role of stratification variables at this level was shown to be slight. But at less aggregative levels, stratification variables may at least partly explain why, in a situation of less than total unionization, a particular individual joins a union and another does not. In other words, the group need to unionize flows from pressures within the work environment itself. But at the margin these pressures might be mediated by the differential impact upon individuals within the group of such aspects of stratification as social imagery, relative deprivation, and status inconsistency.

Stratification variables may also be relevant to a study of union character. The social imagery of union leaders and shop stewards may well be a determinant of union behaviour, just as the membership's social position and imagery may be an impediment or a spur to certain kinds of collective action. The obvious truth that union members and leaders have positions in the social stratification system, and that those positions and the social images which they generate influence their behaviour as unionists, is not being denied. All that is being denied here is the assertion that social stratification constitutes the predominant, or even a major, determinant of union growth and character.

Nor does this study seek to discount the importance of social imagery. Certainly, workers' perceptions of their reality shape their individual and collective behaviour. But images are not necessarily static, limited in number, or holistic in nature. Rather, workers' experience of collective activity can alter their perceptions both of the overall structure of power relationships between groups and the options open to them as collective actors within that structure. All that this study has tried to show is that the models of social imagery used, implicitly or explicitly, by the writers concerned with trade unionism are too simple. The relationship between ideology and behaviour, and between group position and group consciousness, is more complex than their arguments allow.

Nor does this study seek to deny that workers, both manual and white-collar, have at certain times, in certain places, and in certain contexts possessed a class conscious ideology, and that the behaviour of their unions has been motivated by feelings of class solidarity. It has only insisted that such a relationship cannot be assumed to be either automatic or constant. Indeed, by making precisely that assumption, much of the literature surveyed rarely comes to terms with what should be its core evidence: the detailed development through time of a union's goals and behaviour and its membership's social position and perspectives. In consequence, it never confronts the central questions which that historical experience throws up: under which conditions and for which reasons do workers, whether manual or white-collar, come to see themselves as socially connected with interests in common, and under which conditions are those interests perceived to involve a confrontation with the existing social order? In short, all this study has attempted to demonstrate is that the nature of class consciousness must be clearly and explicitly specified, and that this specification must be assessed by its capacity to illuminate the many sided development of trade unionism over time.

If the relationship between social stratification and trade unionism is to be adequately understood, then it must be fitted into a much wider approach to the study of trade unionism. It must begin by recognizing that there are at least four related but analytically distinct questions which any comprehensive theory of the labour movement must consider. These concern the nature and determinants of (a) patterns of union growth, (b) the character of trade unionism, (c) the individual workers' attachment to and participation and involvement in trade unions, and (d) the economic, political, and social consequences of trade unionism.

In answering these questions, there is a need to move

beyond the concepts and the approach generally adopted in the literature considered in earlier chapters. In particular, further study in this area will require more adequate specification of some of the dimensions of unionism itself, and a recognition of the importance of the distribution of social power in constraining the behaviour of individuals and organizations.

Union growth is a relatively unproblematical concept which can be measured relatively easily. But there is a need for a wider and more meaningful specification of union character. Precisely because so much of the literature considered here has operated with too simple a notion of character, it has focused on peripheral aspects of unionism which do not locate the significant points of difference within unions or between them. Unions are not monolithic entities. They exist at many different organizational levels, contain many diverse groups of employees, and operate in many different work and bargaining contexts. Hence propositions about union character must specify to which level, group, or context they refer. Moreover, it must be proved, and not merely assumed, that generalizations about any one of these aspects applies to any or all of the others.

In making comparisons between unions, virtually any dimension of their character is worth considering. But the starting point of the analysis must be a recognition that the basic function of trade unions is participation in job regulation, and that this can be accomplished in different ways. In particular, it is essential that collective bargaining no longer be seen as a unique method of job regulation, but only as one method among many. Indeed, what has to be explained, as an essential element of the study of union character, is why various unions rely more heavily on one system of job regulation than another.

No matter how the concepts of union growth and character are defined, however, they cannot simply be taken as an index of the attitudes and orientations of members or officials towards trade unions or the wider society. Predispositions are not invariably and automatically converted into action. Behaviour is constrained not only by the attitudes of individuals but also by the environment in which it occurs. Indeed, the key to understanding both union growth and character lies in the recognition that each is crucially affected by the distribution of power within which individuals and unions operate, and of which they themselves are a part.

For, as this study has already pointed out, union membership is not necessarily a voluntary act. Individual union members are not totally free to enter or to leave trade unions. Nor, once members, are they necessarily free to shape or to reject union policies adopted in their name. For the union member is in a power relationship with his union no less than with his employer, and his capacity to control or shape union performance cannot be discussed independently of the distribution of sanctions and rewards between the individual and his work group, between the union member and his union bureaucracy, and between the union, his employer, and the state.

What is being suggested here is that possibly union growth can more fruitfully be explained by concentrating on the properties of trade unions as organizations rather than on the properties of the individuals or groups which they seek to organize. In other words, the growth of union membership may turn on those properties which equip the union with power over its members. And more specifically, in the absence of legal enforcement or of other direct state promotion of union membership, union growth becomes predominantly a function of union participation in job regulation. For the various services and benefits which unions are able to offer their members derive primarily from the unions' participation in job regulation, that is, in the making and applying of rules to employment relationships. If union growth is seen in this way, then the study of it is pulled towards a consideration of the distribution of power that permits or prevents union involvement in the processes of job regulation.

Here the study of union growth meets that of union character. For an adequate study of union character must explain the form of job regulation in which the union is engaged, the issues regulated, the level at which they are regulated, and the strategies and tactics used by the union in the process of job regulation. In addition, a full study of union character would also have to analyse the issues at stake, the structure of decision making, and the pattern of rule enforcement in the relationships between the union and its members and the union and the state. In each case, this could not be adequately done without a full consideration of the distribution of sanctions and rewards between the actors involved.*

In other words, the determinants of union growth and character might most productively be identified in the power relationships which surround union activity. Yet paradoxically, if power is seen to stratify society into groups, then the way is open for a reconsideration of the relationship between social stratification and trade unionism.

* The argument expressed in the above three paragraphs owes a great deal to the ideas of Allan Flanders. And it is being refined and tested by work on trade union growth and behaviour which is currently underway at the Industrial Relations Research Unit at the University of Warwick.

Bibliography

1. Acton Society Trust, *Management Succession*, London: The Trust, 1956.
2. Alexander, K. J. W., 'Membership Participation in a Printing Trade Union', *Sociological Review*, II (December, 1954), 161–68.
3. Allen, V. L. 'White-Collar Revolt?' *Listener*, LXVI (30 November 1961), 895–97.
4. ——, 'Trade Unions in Contemporary Capitalism', *The Socialist Register 1964*, Ralph Miliband and John Saville, editors. London: Merlin Press, 1964, pp. 157–74.
5. ——, *Militant Trade Unionism*, London: Merlin Press, 1966.
6. ——, and Sheila Williams, 'The Growth of Trade Unionism in Banking', *Manchester School of Economics and Social Studies*, XXVIII (September, 1960), 299–318.
7. Ashenfelter, Orley, and John H. Pencavel, 'American Trade Union Growth: 1900–1960', *Quarterly Journal of Economics*, LXXXIII (August, 1969), 434–48.
8. Bain, George Sayers, *The Growth of White-Collar Unionism*, Oxford: Clarendon Press, 1970.
9. ——, and R. J. Price, 'Union Growth and Employment Trends in the United Kingdom, 1964–1970', *British Journal of Industrial Relations*, X (November, 1972), 366–81.
10. ——, and R. J. Price, 'Who Is a White-Collar Employee?', *British Journal of Industrial Relations*, X (November, 1972), 325–39.
11. Banks, J. A., *Industrial Participation*, Liverpool: Liverpool University Press, 1963.
12. Barber, Bernard, *Social Stratification*, New York: Harcourt, Brace & World, 1957.
13. Ben-David, Joseph, 'Professions in the Class System of Present-Day Societies: A Trend Report and Bibliography', *Current Sociology*, XII (1963–64), 247–330.
14. ——, 'Professionals and Unions in Israel', *Industrial Relations*, V (October, 1965), 47–66.
15. Blackburn, R. M., *Union Character and Social Class*, London: Batsford, 1967.

16. Blackburn, R. M., and K. Prandy, 'White-Collar Unionization: A Conceptual Framework', *British Journal of Sociology*, XVI (June, 1965), 111–22.

17. ——, K. Prandy, and A. Stewart, 'White-Collar Associations: Organisational Character and Employee Involvement', *Social Stratification and Industrial Relations*, Michael Mann, editor. Proceedings of a Social Science Research Council Conference, Cambridge, 1968. London: The Council, 1969, pp. 86–104.

18. Blum, Albert A., *Management and the White-Collar Union*, New York: American Management Association, 1964.

19. Bott, Elizabeth, *Family and Social Network*, Second edition. London: Tavistock, 1971.

20. Bottomore, T. B., *Classes in Modern Society*, London: Allen & Unwin, 1965.

21. Bowen, Peter, and Monica Shaw, 'Patterns of White-Collar Unionization in the Steel Industry', *Industrial Relations Journal*, III (Summer, 1972), 8–34.

22. Box, Steven, and Stephen Cotgrove, 'Scientific Identity, Occupational Selection, and Role Strain', *British Journal of Sociology*, XVII (March, 1966), 20–8.

23. Brown, Kenneth, 'Sub-Postmasters: Private Traders and Trade Unionists', *British Journal of Industrial Relations*, III (March, 1965), 31–45.

24. Brown, Richard, and Peter Brannen, 'Social Relations and Social Perspectives Amongst Shipbuilding Workers: A Preliminary Statement', *Sociology*, IV (January, 1970), 71–84; (May, 1970), 197–211.

25. ——, P. Brannen, J. M. Cousins, and M. L. Samphier, 'The Contours of Solidarity: Social Stratification and Industrial Relations in Shipbuilding', *British Journal of Industrial Relations*, X (March, 1972), 12–41.

26. Buchanan, William, and Hadley Cantril, *How Nations See Each Other*. Urbana: University of Illinois Press, 1953.

27. Bucher, Rue, and Anselm Strauss, 'Professions in Process', *American Journal of Sociology*, LXVI (January, 1961), 325–334.

28. Burns, Robert K., 'Unionization of the White Collar Worker', *Personnel Series*, No. 110, American Management Association, 1946. Reprinted in Joseph Shister (ed.), *Readings in Labor Economics and Industrial Relations*, Second edition. Chicago: Lippincott, 1956, pp. 65–75

29. ——, 'The White Collar Worker in the American Economy', *Developments in Office Personnel Administration*, No. 127, 1949, pp. 22–38.

30. Butler, David, and Donald Stokes, *Political Change in Britain*, London: Macmillan, 1969.

31. Caplow, Theodore, *The Sociology of Work*, New York: McGraw-Hill, 1954.

32. Carr-Saunders, A. M., and P. A. Wilson, *The Professions*, Ox-

ford: Oxford University Press, 1933. Reprinted by Frank Cass, 1964.

33. Chinoy, Ely, *Automobile Workers and the American Dream*, Garden City, N.Y.: Doubleday, 1955.

34. Clark, James M., *Teachers and Politics in France*, New York: Syracuse University Press, 1967.

35. Clegg, H. A., Alan Fox, and A. F. Thompson, *A History of British Trade Unions Since 1889*, Vol. I, 1889–1910. Oxford: Clarendon Press, 1964.

36. Coates, R. D., *Teachers' Unions and Interest Group Politics*, Cambridge: Cambridge University Press, 1972.

37. Cogan, Morris L., 'The Problem of Defining a Profession', *Annals of the American Academy of Political and Social Science*, CCXCVII (January, 1955), 105–11.

38. Commons, John R., *et al.*, *History of Labour in the United States*, New York: Macmillan, 1918.

39. Cotgrove, Stephen, and Steven Box, *Science, Industry and Society*, London: Allen & Unwin, 1970.

40. ——, and C. Vamplew, 'Technology, Class and Politics: The Case of the Process Workers', *Sociology*, VI (May, 1972), 169–85.

41. Cousins, Jim, 'The Non-Militant Shop Steward', *New Society*, (3 February 1972), 226–28.

42. Craven, John V., 'A Strike of Self-Employed Professionals: Belgian Doctors in 1964', *Industrial and Labor Relations Review*, XXI (October, 1967), 18–31.

43. Crozier, Michel, 'White-Collar Unions: The Case of France', *White-Collar Trade Unions*, Adolf Sturmthal, editor, Urbana: University of Illinois Press, 1966, pp. 90–126.

44. ——, *The World of the Office Worker*, Trans. David Landau, Chicago: University of Chicago Press, 1971.

45. Curtis, Richard F., 'Note on Occupational Mobility and Union Membership in Detroit: A Replication', *Social Forces*, XXXVIII (October, 1959), 69–71.

46. Cyriax, George, and Robert Oakeshott, 'White-Collar Unions', *The Bargainers*, London: Faber, 1960, pp. 141–61.

47. Dahrendorf, Ralf, *Class and Class Conflict in an Industrial Society*, London: Routledge & Kegan Paul, 1959.

48. ——, *Conflict After Class: New Perspectives on the Theory of Social and Political Conflict*, London: Longmans for the University of Essex, 1967.

49. Dale, J. R., *The Clerk in Industry*, Liverpool: Liverpool University Press, 1962.

50. Daniel, W. W., 'Industrial Behaviour and Orientation to Work: A Critique', *Journal of Management Studies*, VI (October, 1969), 366–75.

51. ——, 'Productivity Bargaining and Orientation to Work: A Rejoinder to Goldthorpe', *Journal of Management Studies*, VIII (October, 1971), 329–35.

52. Davies, A. F., 'Prestige of Occupations', *British Journal of Sociology*, III (June, 1952), 134–47.

53. Dean, Lois R., 'Union Activity and Dual Loyalty', *Industrial and Labor Relations Review*, VII (July, 1954), 526–36.

54. Downey, E. H., 'Introduction', *Trade Unionism in the United States*, R. F. Hoxie, Second edition, New York: Appleton, 1923. Reprinted by Russell and Russell of New York, 1966, pp. xiii-xxxiii.

55. Dufty, N. F., 'The White Collar Unionist', *Journal of Industrial Relations*, III (October, 1961), 151–56.

56. ——, 'White Collar Contrast', *International Journal of Comparative Sociology*, IV, (March, 1963), 64–73.

57. Dvorak, Eldon J., 'Will Engineers Unionize?' *Industrial Relations*, II, (May, 1963), 45–65.

58. Eckstein, H., 'The Politics of the British Medical Association', *Political Quarterly*, XXVI (May, 1955), 345–59.

59. ——, *Pressure Group Politics*, London: Allen & Unwin, 1960.

60. Edwards, Alba M., *A Social-Economic Grouping of the Gainful Workers of the United States*, Washington: United States Government Printing Office, 1938.

61. Eisenstadt, S. N., 'Prestige, Participation and Strata Formation', *Social Stratification*, J. A. Jackson, editor, Cambridge: Cambridge University Press, 1968, pp. 62–103.

62. Ellis, N. D., *The Scientific Worker: The Study of Qualified Scientists and Engineers Employed in Government and Industrial Research Establishments*, unpublished Ph.d. thesis, University of Leeds, 1969.

63. Ellis, Valerie A., *Some Sociological Dimensions of Unionisation Among Technical and Supervisory Employees*, unpublished Ph.d. thesis, University of Leeds, 1971.

64. Fivelsdal, Egil, 'White-Collar Unions and the Norwegian Labor Movement', *Industrial Relations*, V (October, 1965), 80–92.

65. Flanders, Allan, 'Movement in Unions', *New Society*, (11 February 1965), 15–17.

66. ——, *Industrial Relations: What Is Wrong With the System?*, London: Faber, 1965.

67. ——, 'Trade Unions and Politics', *Management and Unions*, London: Faber, 1970, pp. 24–37.

68. Floud, Jean, 'The Educational Experience of the Adult Population of England and Wales as at July 1949', *Social Mobility in Britain*, D. Glass, editor, London: Routledge & Kegan Paul, 1954, pp. 98–140.

69. Foote, Nelson N., 'The Professionalization of Labor in Detroit', *American Journal of Sociology*, LVIII (January, 1953), 371–80.

70. Fughrig, Wolf D., 'A Quasi-Union: West German University Association', *Industrial Relations*, V (October, 1965), 116–27.

71. Gallup Poll, *Trade Unions and the Public in 1964*, London: Gallup Poll, 1964.

72. Gerth, H. H. and C. Wright Mills (trans.), *From Max Weber:*

Essays In Sociology, London: Routledge & Kegan Paul, 1948.
73. Gilb, Corinne Lathrop, *Hidden Hierarchies: The Professions and Government*, New York: Harper & Row, 1966.
74. Glantz, Oscar, 'Class Consciousness and Political Solidarity', *American Sociological Review*, XXIII (August, 1958), 375–83.
75. Goffman, Irving W., 'Status Consistency and Preference for Change in Power Distribution', *American Sociological Review*, XXII (June, 1957), 275–81.
76. Goldstein, Bernard, 'Unions and the Professional Employee', *Journal of Business*, XXVII (October, 1954), 276–84.
77. ——, 'Some Aspects of the Nature of Unionism Among Salaried Professionals in Industry', *American Sociological Review*, XX (April, 1955), 199–205.
78. ——, *Unions for Technical Professionals: A Case Study*, unpublished Ph.d. thesis, University of Chicago, 1957.
79. ——, 'The Perspective of Unionized Professionals', *Social Forces*, XXXVII (May, 1959), 323–27.
80. ——, and Bernard P. Indik, 'Unionism as a Social Choice: The Engineers' Case', *Monthly Labor Review*, LXXXVI (April, 1963), 365–69.
81. Goldthorpe, John H., 'Attitudes and Behaviour of Car Assembly Workers: A Deviant Case and a Theoretical Critique', *British Journal of Sociology*, XVII (September, 1966), 227–44.
82. ——, 'The Social Action Approach to Industrial Sociology: A Reply to Daniel', *Journal of Management Studies*, VII (May, 1970), 199–208.
83. ——, 'Daniel on Orientations to Work: A Final Comment', *Journal of Management Studies*, IX (October, 1972), 266–73.
84. ——, and David Lockwood, 'Affluence and the British Class Structure', *Sociological Review*, XI (July, 1963), 133–63.
85. ——, David Lockwood, Frank Bechhofer, and Jennifer Platt, 'The Affluent Worker and the Thesis of Embourgeoisement: Some Preliminary Research Findings', *Sociology*, I (January, 1967), 11–31.
86. ——, *The Affluent Worker: Industrial Attitudes and Behaviour*, Cambridge: Cambridge University Press, 1968.
87. ——, *The Affluent Worker: Political Attitudes and Behaviour*, Cambridge: Cambridge University Press, 1968.
88. ——, *The Affluent Worker in the Class Structure*, Cambridge: Cambridge University Press, 1969.
89. Goode, William J., 'Community Within a Community: The Professions', *American Sociological Review*, XXII (April, 1957), 194–200.
90. Gordon, Milton M., *Social Class in American Sociology*, New York: McGraw-Hill, 1950.
91. Grant, Andrew, *Socialism and the Middle Classes*, London: Lawrence & Wishart, 1958.
92. Grunfeld, Cyril, *Modern Trade Union Law*, London: Sweet & Maxwell, 1966.

93. Guttman, Louis, 'A Basis for Scaling Qualitative Data', *American Sociological Review*, IX (April, 1944), 139–50.

94. Great Britain, *Report of a Court of Inquiry Under Lord Pearson into the Dispute Between the British Steel Corporation and Certain of Their Employees*, London: H.M.S.O., 1968, Cmnd. 3754.

95. ——, *Report of the Royal Commission on Trade Unions and Employers' Associations*, London: H.M.S.O., 1968, Cmnd. 3623.

96. Habenstein, Robert W., 'Critique of "Profession" as a Sociological Category', *Sociological Quarterly*, IV (Autumn, 1963), 291–300.

97. Hall, John, and D. Caradog Jones, 'Social Grading of Occupations', *British Journal of Sociology*, I (March, 1950), 31–55.

98. Hall, Richard H., 'Some Organizational Considerations in the Professional–Organizational Relationship', *Administrative Science Quarterly*, XII (December, 1967), 461–78.

99. ——, 'Professionalization and Bureaucratization', *American Sociological Review*, XXXIII (February, 1968), 92–104.

100. Hamilton, Richard F., 'The Marginal Middle Class: A Reconsideration', *American Sociological Review*, XXXI (April, 1966), 192–99.

101. Harrison, Martin, *Trade Unions and the Labour Party Since 1945*, London: Allen & Unwin, 1960.

102. Hartfiel, Gunter, 'Germany', *White-Collar Trade Unions*, Adolf Sturmthal, editor, Urbana: University of Illinois Press, 1966, pp. 127–64.

103. Hatt, Paul, K., 'Occupation and Social Stratification', *American Journal of Sociology*, LV (May, 1950), 533–43.

104. Hickson, D. J., and M. W. Thomas, 'Professionalization in Britain: A Preliminary Measurement', *Sociology*, III (January, 1969), 37–53.

105. Hill, Stephen, 'Dockers and Their Work', *New Society* (17 August 1972), 338–40.

106. Hindell, Keith, *Trade Union Membership*, London: Political and Economic Planning, 1962.

107. Hines, A. G., 'Trade Unions and Wage Inflation in the United Kingdom, 1893–1961', *Review of Economic Studies*, XXXI (October, 1964), 221–52.

108. ——, 'Wage Inflation in the United Kingdom, 1948–1962: A Disaggregated Study', *Economic Journal*, LXXIX (March, 1969), 66–89.

109. Hobsbawm, E. J., 'The Labour Aristocracy in Nineteenth Century Britain', *Labouring Men*, London, Weidenfeld & Nicolson, 1964, pp. 272–315.

110. Hodge, Robert W., Donald J. Treiman, and Peter H. Rossi, 'A Comparative Study of Occupational Prestige', *Class, Status, and Power*, Reinhard Bendix and Seymour M. Lipset, editors,

Second edition, London: Routledge & Kegan Paul, 1967, pp. 309–21.

111. Hodge, Robert W., Paul M. Siegel, and Peter H. Rossi, 'Occupational Prestige in the United States: 1925–1963', *Class, Status, and Power*, Reinhard Bendix and Seymour M. Lipset, editors, Second edition, London: Routledge & Kegan Paul, 1967, pp. 322–34.

112. Hoxie, R. F., *Trade Unionism in the United States*, Second edition, New York: Appleton, 1923. Reprinted by Russell and Russell of New York, 1966.

113. Hudson, Ruth Alice, and Hjalmar Rosen, 'Union Political Action: The Member Speaks', *Industrial and Labor Relations Review*, VII (April, 1954), 404–18.

114. Hughes, Everett C., 'The Sociological Study of Work: An Editorial Foreword', *American Journal of Sociology*, LVII (March, 1952), 423–26.

115. ——, 'Professions', *Daedalus*, XCII (Fall, 1963), 655–68.

116. Husaini, Bagar A., and James A. Geschwender, 'Some Correlates of Attitudes Toward and Membership in White-Collar Unions', *South Western Social Science Quarterly*, XLVIII (March, 1968), 595–601.

117. Hyman, Richard, *Marxism and the Sociology of Trade Unionism*, London: Pluto Press, 1971.

118. ——, *Strikes*, London: Fontana/Collins, 1972.

119. Indik, Bernard P., and Bernard Goldstein, 'Professional Engineers Look at Unions', *Proceedings of the Industrial Relations Research Association*, XVI (December, 1963), 209–19.

120. Inkeles, Alex, and Peter H. Rossi, 'National Comparisons of Occupational Prestige', *American Journal of Sociology*, LXI (January, 1956), 329–39.

121. Jackson, J. A., (ed.), *Social Stratification*, Cambridge: Cambridge University Press, 1968.

122. ——, *Professions and Professionalization*, Cambridge: Cambridge University Press, 1970.

123. Kahan, Michael, David Butler, and Donald Stokes, 'On the Analytical Division of Social Class', *British Journal of Sociology*, XVII (June, 1966), 122–32.

124. Kaplan, Norman, 'Professional Scientists in Industry: An Essay Review', *Social Problems*, XIII (Summer, 1965), 88–97.

125. Kassalow, Everett M., 'White-Collar Unionism in Western Europe', *Monthly Labor Review*, LXXXVI (July, 1963), 765–71; (August, 1963), 889–96.

126. ——, 'The Prospects for White-Collar Union Growth', *Industrial Relations*, V (October, 1965), 37–47.

127. ——, 'White-Collar Unionism in the United States', *White-Collar Trade Unions*, Adolf Sturmthal, editor, Urbana: University of Illinois Press, 1966, pp. 305–64.

128. Kassalow, Everett M., 'Professional Unionism in Sweden', *Industrial Relations*, VIII (February, 1969), 119–34.

129. Kelsall, R. K., D. Lockwood, and A. Tropp, 'The New Middle Class in the Power Structure of Great Britain', *Transactions of the Third World Congress of Sociology*, III (1956), 320–29.

130. Kleingartner, Archie, 'Professional Associations: An Alternative to Unions?' *Contemporary Labor Issues*, Walter Fogel and Archie Kleingartner, editors, Belmont, Calif.: Wadsworth, 1966, pp. 249–56.

131. ——, *Professionalism and Salaried Worker Organization*, Madison: University of Wisconsin, Industrial Relations Research Institute, 1967.

132. ——, 'The Organization of White-Collar Workers', *British Journal of Industrial Relations*, VI (March, 1968), 79–93.

133. ——, 'Professionalism and Engineering Unionism', *Industrial Relations*, VIII (May, 1969), 224–35.

134. Klingender, F. D., *The Condition of Clerical Labour in Great Britain*, London: Martin Lawrence, 1935.

135. Kornhauser, Ruth, 'Some Social Determinants and Consequences of Union Membership', *Labor History*, II (Winter, 1961), 30–61.

136. Kornhauser, William, *Scientists in Industry: Conflict and Accommodation*, Berkeley and Los Angeles: University of California Press, 1963.

137. Kuhn, James W., 'Success and Failure in Organizing Professional Engineers', *Proceedings of the Industrial Relations Research Association*, XVI (December, 1963), 194–208.

138. Lakenbacher, Ernst, 'White-Collar Unions in Austria', *White-Collar Trade Unions*, Adolf Sturmthal, editor, Urbana: University of Illinois Press, 1966, pp. 37–89.

139. Landecker, Werner S., 'Class Crystallization and Class Consciousness', *American Sociological Review*, XXVIII (April, 1963), 219–29.

140. Lenski, Gerhard E., 'Status Crystallization: A Non-vertical Dimension of Social Status', *American Sociological Review*, XIX (August, 1954), 405–13.

141. ——, 'Social Participation and Class Crystallization', *American Sociological Review*, XXI (August, 1956), 458–64.

142. Lester, Richard A., *As Unions Mature*, Princeton: Princeton University Press, 1958.

143. Levine, Solomon B., 'The White-Collar Blue-Collar Alliance in Japan', *Industrial Relations*, V (October, 1965), 103–15.

144. ——, 'Unionization of White-Collar Employees in Japan', *White-Collar Trade Unions*, Adolf Sturmthal, editor, Urbana: University of Illinois Press, 1966, pp. 205–60.

145. Lewis, Roy, and Angus Maude, *Professional People*, London: Phoenix House, 1952.

146. ——, *The English Middle Classes*, London: Phoenix House, 1953.

147. Lipset, Seymour M., 'The Future of Non-Manual Unionism'. Unpublished paper, Institute of Industrial Relations, University of California, Berkeley, 1961.

148. ——, 'Trade Unions and Social Structure', *Industrial Relations*, I (October, 1961), 75–90; (February, 1962), 89–110

149. ——, and Joan Gordon, 'Mobility and Trade Union Membership', *Class, Status, and Power*, Reinhard Bendix and Seymour M. Lipset, editors, Glencoe: Free Press, 1953, pp. 491–500.

150. Lockwood, David, *The Blackcoated Worker*, London: Allen & Unwin, 1958.

151. ——, 'The "New Working Class"', *European Journal of Sociology*, I (1960), 248–59.

152. ——, 'Sources of Variation in Working Class Images of Society', *Sociological Review*, XIV (November, 1966), 249–67.

153. Lombardi, Vincent, and Andrew J. Grimes, 'A Primer for a Theory of White-Collar Unionization', *Monthly Labor Review*, XC (May, 1967), 46–49.

154. Lupton, T., *On the Shop Floor*, Oxford: Pergamon, 1963.

155. Manis, Jerome G., and Bernard N. Meltzer, 'Attitudes of Textile Workers to Class Structure', *American Journal of Sociology*, LX (July, 1954), 30–35.

156. Marcson, Simon, *The Scientist in American Industry*, New York: Harper for the Industrial Relations Section, Department of Economics, Princeton University, 1960.

157. Marsh, Arthur, *Industrial Relations in Engineering*, Oxford: Pergamon, 1965.

158. Marshall, T. H., 'The Recent History of Professionalism in Relation to Social Structure and Social Policy', *Citizenship and Social Class*, Cambridge: Cambridge University Press, 1950, pp. 128–55.

159. Martin, R. M., 'Australian Professional and White-Collar Unions', *Industrial Relations*, V (October, 1965), 93–102.

160. ——, 'Class Identification and Trade Union Behaviour: The Case of Australian Whitecollar Unions', *Journal of Industrial Relations*, VII (July, 1965), 131–48.

161 ——, *Whitecollar Unions in Australia*, Sydney: Australian Institute of Political Science, 1965.

162. Maurice, Marc, Colette Monteil, Roland Guillon, and Jacqueline Gaulon, *Les Cadres et L'Entreprise*, Paris: Universite de Paris, Institut des Sciences Sociales du Travail, 1967.

163. McCarthy, W. E. J., 'Why Workers Join Unions', *New Society* (26 October 1967), 599.

164. McCormick, Brian, 'Managerial Unionism in the Coal Industry', *British Journal of Sociology*, XI (December, 1960), 356–69.

165. McKenzie, Robert, and Allan Silver, *Angels in Marble*, London: Heinemann, 1968.

166. Mercer, D. E., and D. T. H. Weir, 'Orientations to Work Among White-Collar Workers', *Social Stratification and Industrial Relations*, Michael Mann, editor. Proceedings of a Social Science Research Council Conference, Cambridge, 1968. London: The Council, 1969, pp. 112–45.

167. ——, 'Attitudes to Work and Trade Unionism Among White-Collar Workers', *Industrial Relations Journal*, III (Summer, 1972), 49–60.

168. Millerson, Geoffrey, *The Qualifying Associations*, London: Routledge & Kegan Paul, 1964.

169. Mills, C. Wright, 'Notes on White-Collar Unionism', *Labor and Nation*, V (March–April, 1949), 17–21; (May–June, 1949), 17–20.

170. ——, *White Collar*, New York: Oxford University Press, 1951.

171. Mortimer, J. E., *A History of the Association of Engineering and Shipbuilding Draughtsmen*, London: The Association, 1960.

172. Muir J. Douglas, 'The Strike as a Professional Sanction: The Changing Attitude of the National Education Association', *Labor Law Journal*, XIX (October, 1968), 615–27.

173. Nilstein, Arne H., 'White-Collar Unionism in Sweden', *White-Collar Trade Unions*, Adolf Sturmthal, editor, Urbana: University of Illinois Press, 1966, pp. 261–304.

174. Nordlinger, Eric A., *The Working-Class Tories*, London: MacGibbon & Kee, 1967.

175. North, C. C., and P. K. Hatt, 'Jobs and Occupations', *Class, Status, and Power*, Reinhard Bendix and Seymour M. Lipset, editors, Glencoe: Free Press, 1953, pp. 411–26.

176. Olson, Mancur, 'The Labor Union and Economic Freedom', *The Logic of Collective Action*, Cambridge, Mass.: Harvard University Press, 1965, pp. 66–97.

177. Ossowski, Stanislaw, *Class Structure in the Social Consciousness*, London: Routledge & Kegan Paul, 1963.

178. Owen, Carol, *Social Stratification*, London: Routledge & Kegan Paul, 1968.

179. Phillipson, Charles Michael, *A Study of the Attitudes Towards and Participation in Trade Union Activities of Selected Groups of Non-Manual Workers*, unpublished M.A. thesis, University of Nottingham, 1964.

180. Pickard, O. G., 'Clerical Workers and the Trade Unions', *British Management Review*, XIII (April, 1955), 102–20.

181. Pickles, William, 'Trade Unions in the Political Climate', *Industrial Relations: Contemporary Problems and Perspectives*, B. C. Roberts, editor, Revised edition, London: Methuen, 1968, pp. 257–94.

182. Plamenatz, John, *Ideology*, London: Macmillan, 1971.

183. Popitz, Heinrich, *et al.*, *Das Gesellschaftsbild des Arbeiters*, Tubingen: J. C. B. Mohr (Paul Siebeck), 1957.

184. Prandy, Kenneth, *Professional Employees*, London: Faber, 1965.

185. Prandy, Kenneth, 'Professional Organization in Great Britain', *Industrial Relations*, V (October, 1965), 67–79.

186. Purcell, Theodore V., *Blue Collar Man*, Cambridge, Mass.: Harvard University Press, 1960.

187. Rawson, D. W., 'The Frontiers of Trade Unionism', *Australian Journal of Politics and History*, I (May, 1956), 196–209.

188. Rex, John, *Key Problems of Sociological Theory*, London: Routledge & Kegan Paul, 1961.

189. Réynaud, Jean-Daniel, 'Stratification and Industrial Relations: Reflections on the Trade Unionism of Blackcoated, Technical and Managerial Employees', *Social Stratification and Industrial Relations*, Michael Mann, editor. Proceedings of a Social Science Research Council Conference, Cambridge, 1968, London: The Council, 1969, pp. 147–60.

190. Ridley, F. F., *Revolutionary Syndicalism in France*, Cambridge: Cambridge University Press, 1970.

191. Riegel, J. W., *Collective Bargaining as Viewed by Unorganized Engineers and Scientists*, Ann Arbor: University of Michigan, Bureau of Industrial Relations, 1959.

192. Ritti, Richard, 'Work Goals of Scientists and Engineers', *Industrial Relations*, VII (February, 1968), 118–31.

193. Rose, Arnold M., *Union Solidarity*, Minneapolis: University of Minnesota Press, 1952.

194. Routh, Guy, 'The Social Co-ordinates of Design Technicians', *The Draughtsman* (September, 1961), 7–10.

195. ——, 'White-Collar Unions in the United Kingdom', *White-Collar Trade Unions*, Adolf Sturmthal, editor, Urbana: University of Illinois Press, 1966, pp. 165–204.

196. Runciman, W. G., *Relative Deprivation and Social Justice*, London: Routledge & Kegan Paul, 1966.

197. ——, 'Class, Status, and Power?', *Sociology in Its Place and Other Essays*, Cambridge: Cambridge University Press, 1970, pp. 102–40.

198. Samuel, R., 'The Deference Voter', *New Left Review*, No. 1 (January–February, 1960), 9–13.

199. Schneider, Eugene V., 'Theories of the Labor Movement', *Industrial Sociology*, New York: McGraw-Hill, 1957, pp. 331–49.

200. Scott, W. Richard, 'Professionals in Bureaucracies: Areas of Conflict', *Professionalization*, Howard M. Vollmer and Donald L. Mills, editors, Englewood Cliffs, N.J.: Prentice-Hall, 1966, pp. 265–75.

201. Segerstedt, Torgny T., 'An Investigation of Class-Consciousness Among Office Employees and Workers in Swedish Factories', *Transactions of the Second World Congress of Sociology*, II (1954), 298–308.

202. Seidman, Joel, and Glen G. Cain, 'Unionized Engineers and Chemists: A Case Study of a Professional Union', *Journal of Business*, XXXVII (July, 1964), 238–57.

203. Seidman, Joel, Jack London and Bernard Karsh, 'Political Consciousness in a Local Union', *Public Opinion Quarterly*, XV (Winter, 1951–52), 692–702.

204. Shlakman, Vera, 'White Collar Unions and Professional Organizations', *Science and Society*, XIV (March, 1950), 214–36.

205. ——, 'Unionism and Professional Organizations Among Engineers', *Science and Society*, XIV (April, 1950), 322–37.

206. ——, 'Business and the Salaried Worker', *Science and Society*, XV (1951), 97–121.

207. ——, 'Status and Ideology of Office Workers', *Science and Society*, XVI (1951), 1–26.

208. Shostack, Arthur B., *America's Forgotten Labor Organization*, Princeton: Princeton University, Department of Economics, Industrial Relations Section, 1962.

209. ——, and William Gomberg (eds.), *Blue-Collar World: Studies of the American Worker*, Englewood Cliffs, N.J.: Prentice-Hall, 1964.

210. Silverman, David, 'Clerical Ideologies: A Research Note', *British Journal of Sociology*, XIX (September, 1968), 326–33.

211. Simpson, Richard L., and Ida Harper Simpson, 'Correlates and Estimation of Occupational Prestige', *American Journal of Sociology*, LXVI (September, 1960), 135–40.

212. Social Surveys (Gallup Poll) Limited, *Gallup Poll on the Trade Unions: Undertaken for the News Chronicle*, London: Social Surveys (Gallup Poll) Ltd., 1959.

213. Soffer, Benson, 'A Theory of Trade Union Development: The Role of the "Autonomous" Workman', *Labor History*, I (Spring, 1960), 141–63.

214. Solomon, Benjamin, and Robert K. Burns, 'Unionization of White-Collar Employees: Extent, Potential, and Implications', *Journal of Business*, XXXVI (April, 1963), 141–65.

215. Spinrad, William, 'Correlates of Trade Union Participation: A Summary of the Literature', *American Sociological Review*, XXV (April, 1960), 237–44.

216. Stagner, Ross, 'Foreword', *Blue Collar Man*, Theodore V. Purcell, Cambridge, Mass.: Harvard University Press, 1960, pp. vii–ix.

217. Strauss, George, 'White-Collar Unions Are Different!', *Harvard Business Review*, XXXII (September–October, 1954), 73–82.

218. ——, 'Professionalism and Occupational Associations', *Industrial Relations*, II (May, 1963), 7–31.

219. ——, 'Professional or Employee-Oriented: Dilemma for Engineering Unions', *Industrial and Labor Relations Review*, XVII (July, 1964), 519–33.

220. ——, 'The AAUP as a Professional Occupational Association', *Industrial Relations*, V (October, 1965), 128–40.

221. Sturmthal, Adolf, 'White-Collar Unions: A Comparative Essay', *White-Collar Trade Unions*, Urbana: University of Illinois Press, 1966, pp. 365–98.

222. Sykes, A. J. M., 'The Problem of Clerical Trade Unionism', *Scientific Business*, II (August, 1964), 176–83.
223. ——, 'Some Differences in the Attitudes of Clerical and of Manual Workers', *Sociological Review*, XIII (November, 1965), 297–310.
224. ——, 'Attitudes to Political Affiliation in a Printing Trade Union', *Scottish Journal of Political Economy*, XII (June, 1965), 161–179.
225. ——, 'The Cohesion of a Trade Union Workshop Organization', *Sociology*, I (May, 1967), 141–63.
226. ——, 'Navvies: Their Work Attitudes', *Sociology*, III (January, 1969), 21–35.
227. ——, 'Navvies: Their Social Relations', *Sociology*, III (May, 1969), 157–72.
228. Taylor, Lee, *Occupational Sociology*, New York: Oxford University Press, 1968.
229. Troy, Leo, 'Local Independent and National Unions: Competitive Labor Organizations', *Journal of Political Economy*, LXVIII (October, 1960), 487–506.
230. ——, *Local Independent Unionism: Two Case Studies*, New Brunswick, N.J.: Rutgers University, Institute of Management and Labor Relations, 1961.
231. ——, 'Local Independent Unions and the American Labor Movement', *Industrial and Labor Relations Review*, XIV (April, 1961), 331–49.
232. ——, *Trade Union Membership, 1897–1962*, New York: National Bureau of Economic Research, 1965.
233. Tucker, C. W., 'On Working Class Identification', *American Sociological Review*, XXXI (December, 1966), 855–56, See also No. 100.
234. Turner, H. A., *Trade Union Growth, Structure and Policy*, London: Allen & Unwin, 1962.
235. Ulman, Lloyd, *The Rise of the National Trade Union*, Cambridge, Mass.: Harvard University Press, 1955.
236. Veblen, Thorstein, *The Engineers and the Price System*, New York: Harcourt, Brace & World, 1963.
237. Volker, D., 'NALGO's Affiliation to the T.U.C.', *British Journal of Industrial Relations*, IV (March, 1966), 59–76.
238. Vollmer, Howard M., and Donald L. Mills, 'Some Comments on the Professionalization of Everyone?', *American Journal of Sociology*, LXX (January, 1965), 480–81. See also No. 244.
239. —— (eds.), *Professionalization*, Englewood Cliffs, N.J.: Prentice-Hall, 1966.
240. Walker, K. F., 'White-collar Unionism in Australia', *White-Collar Trade Unions*, Adolf Sturmthal, editor, Urbana: University of Illinois Press, 1966, pp. 1–36.
241. Walton, Richard E., *The Impact of the Professional Engineering Union*, Boston: Harvard University, Division of Research, 1961.

242. Webb, Sidney and Beatrice, *The History of Trade Unionism*, London: Longmans Green, 1920.

243. Westergaard, J. H., 'The Rediscovery of the Cash Nexus', *The Socialist Register 1970*, Ralph Miliband and John Saville, editors, London: Merlin Press, 1970, pp. 111–38.

244. Wilensky, Harold L., 'The Professionalization of Everyone?', *American Journal of Sociology*, LXX (September, 1964), 137–58.

245. ——, 'Class, Class Consciousness and American Workers', *Labor in a Changing America*, William Haber, editor, New York: Basic Books, 1966, pp. 12–44.

246. Willener, Alfred, *Images de la Société et Classes Sociales*, Berne, 1957.

247. Woodward, Joan, 'We're All Bourgeois Now', *New Society* (25 July 1968), 132–3. See reply by Bechhofer, *et al.*, *New Society* (1 August 1968), 172–3.

248. Wootton, Barbara, *The Social Foundations of Wage Policy*, New York: Norton, 1955.

249. Wootton, Graham, 'Parties in Union Government: The AESD', *Political Studies*, IX (June, 1961), 141–56.

250. ——, 'A Technicians' Trade Union', *New Society* (4 July 1963), 13–15.

251. Worsley, Peter, *et al.*, *Introducing Sociology*, Hardmondsworth, Middlesex: Penguin, 1970.

252. Young, Michael, and Peter Willmott, 'Social Grading by Manual Workers', *British Journal of Sociology*, VII (December, 1956), 337–45.